When Tricia's book found me, I was—*I am!*—in a season of waiting. Unexpected, unchosen, unwanted waiting. And in the pages of *Just. You. Wait.*, I discovered a good guide who's weathered waiting with God, in all its comfort and discomfort. This book is a gift to all of us who are a little peeved and disheartened by the wait, because in its pages, we discover we're not alone.

MARGOT STARBUCK, author of *Small Things with Great Love*

Tricia's ability to simultaneously strike and soothe the human heart is nothing short of extraordinary. I wasn't particularly struggling with impatience when I turned to the first page of *Just. You. Wait.*—or so I thought. But I needed this book. With raw authenticity and quirky humor, Tricia avoids offering trite answers to unanswerable heartaches and instead shares quiet, poignant insights that make you suck in your breath deeply— and ponder and wrestle and shift. As I face my own season of waiting, with patience and hope sorely lacking in my own soul, I am grateful for the gift of Tricia, who has gone before me and paved the way. I am not the same for having read these pages.

SEPTEMBER VAUDREY, author of *Colors of Goodbye*

Tricia Lott Williford has created something special here, something true. If you have ever been in a difficult waiting season or are walking with someone through a painful life stage, you will find a soul companion here. With her signature humor (yes, testicles are mentioned more than once) and vulnerability, *Just. You. Wait.* is not a how-to book or a book of trite answers— as we see so often from books in these categories. Instead, Lott Williford holds raw courage in one hand and real heartbreak in the other, while offering it all as a gift to the reader. Unwrap this gift, reader. You will be grateful you did.

AUBREY SAMPSON, author of *The Louder Song* and *Overcomer*

Modern Western culture, with its blurring advances, has tried to jettison our need to wait for anything. That's why this book is so important. By bringing us into her own family's story, Tricia Lott Williford reminds us that waiting is a good thing. With candidness and humor, *Just. You. Wait.* points the way to the many hidden treasures that lie ahead for those who embrace a lifestyle of patience, hardy laughter, and stubborn hope.

JASON HAGUE, author of *Aching Joy*

Reading Tricia's writing is like sharing a cup of coffee with your best friend or sister—her experiences speak wisdom into your own. Waiting is a natural part of life, but it's one that we don't like. We pretend that it doesn't exist—but it does, and we must be ready for it. In *Just. You. Wait.*, Tricia beautifully and winsomely shows us the value in waiting.

CATHERINE MCNIEL, author of *Long Days of Small Things* and *All Shall Be Well*

Tricia is the most compassionate writer I have ever read. She forges a sincere friendship with the reader, writing as a tender survivor of waiting rather than an expert on it. Somehow, Tricia manages to strike the perfect balance between consolation and hope, nudging us forward without hurrying us along. For those who feel stuck, sidelined, or distracted by the ache of longing, *Just. You. Wait.* offers the solace and perspective you need. That's exactly what it gave to me.

BEKAH DIFELICE, author of *Almost There*

Just. You. Wait.

ON WAITING WELL

474

F60

THANK
YOU
FOR
WAITING

Just. You. Wait.

*Patience, Contentment, and
Hope for the Everyday*

TRICIA LOTT WILLIFORD

NavPress

A NavPress resource published in alliance
with Tyndale House Publishers, Inc.

NavPress ◑

NavPress is the publishing ministry of The Navigators, an international Christian organization and leader in personal spiritual development. NavPress is committed to helping people grow spiritually and enjoy lives of meaning and hope through personal and group resources that are biblically rooted, culturally relevant, and highly practical.

For more information, visit www.NavPress.com.

For Peter,

my favorite.

Maybe

the best thing

I've ever done

was wait.

I made an art form

out of

endurance.

You were worth

every single

moment.

Tyler Knott Gregson

Contents

Hurry Up and Wait

I start the morning with such a friendly disposition. I promise you, I do.

"Good morning, guys," I say with my gentle morning voice. I scratch their backs as they stir and open their eyes. I even give each of them morning warnings: "You don't have to get up quite yet, but pretty soon. You can sleep a little longer, lovey."

I'm telling you: I do not wake up in a grumpy mood. I don't even think I have "the wrong side of the bed." (Unless I am awakened by a screeching, buzzing alarm. Then all bets are off.) But generally, I am of a fine disposition in the morning. I come downstairs, always wrapped in my robe, my hair still wayward and wild. I sit in a central location, I drink the morning cup of coffee, and I supervise the happenings.

And then things slowly slip sideways.

"Buddy, could you get dressed before you have your breakfast?"

"I see you have a shirt on, but I need you to wear pants also."

"I put your milk on your Cocoa Pebbles, so it can start to get soggy." (Never mind that it's against human nature to like soggy cereal. I'm a professional, and I choose my battles.)

"Would you like for me to pack your lunch today, or do you want to pack it?"

"Could you please come to the table?"

"Please don't be silly at the table."

"Stop picking fights with your brother."

"No, your chocolate milk doesn't taste like coffee. It's not coffee. No, I promise you: It is not coffee."

"We are leaving in twelve minutes. Have you packed your lunch? You said you wanted to be in charge of your lunch today."

"It. Is. Not. Coffee."

"Remember to brush your teeth, please."

"Only two cookies in your lunch."

"Only two cookies, I said."

"Two cookies."

"Your chocolate milk does not have coffee in it. Seriously. I promise."

"I know you need a snack also, and you can choose grapes or goldfish crackers. No, the cookies are for your lunch—actually, you can eat the cookies any time you want throughout the day. But you are not taking more than two cookies to school in any part of your lunch or backpack."

"Have you brushed your teeth? No, we brush at night to keep our teeth. We brush in the morning to keep our friends."

"Shoes and socks, please."

"We're leaving in seven minutes."

"Shoes and socks, please."

"Shoes. And socks. What is your job right now? That's right. Do it."

"Two cookies is the limit. I'm not changing my mind on this."

"There is No. Coffee. In. Your. Chocolate. Milk."

"Shoes."

"We're leaving in two minutes."

"Don't forget to fill your water bottle."

"Buddy. Shoes."

"We are leaving ten seconds ago."

And then: *Enough.*

"You guys! Shoes and socks *on*! I told you—two cookies and *only two cookies*! And for crying out loud, *I did not* put coffee in your milk! Put your lunch in your backpack and *get in the CAR!*"

And then they look at me with weepy, hurting eyes. "Mom, why do you have to be so angry in the morning?"

I read somewhere that there is no grace in hurrying. But sometimes grace has been patient for as long as she could.

No matter how well I start out the morning, the small bits of waiting chip away at the good intentions in my day. Time and people move too slowly, making me feel impatient or ignored. Things don't work out like they should, or they don't work out at all—and suddenly I'm slamming the dishwasher and rushing the kids. My everyday inconveniences are nothing in comparison to the greater sufferings happening in the world, and yet they are not nothing. They are my world, petty as it sometimes feels. Waiting fills up my ordinary days.

Waiting turns me into someone I don't want to be. It changes me in small ways and big ones, from the edge in my voice to the lasting lessons I teach my children by my lousy example.

The challenges of waiting are familiar to all of us. Everybody waits. Nobody likes it. It's part of life, part of every single day.

We wait in line, wait for coffee to percolate, wait for the light to change, wait for Christmas, wait for morning, wait for permission.

We wait for a spouse, wait for a baby, wait on our children, wait on our parents.

We wait in the doctor's office, in the dentist's office, in the post office, and for a leader to take office.

We wait for clarity, for direction, to feel sure.

We wait on a job, a promotion, a new boss, a new day.

We wait for hope and for healing and for miracles.

We wait on God. And when we misunderstand what waiting is about, we can get confused about what God is up to.

Waiting is a big deal to God. It's one of God's favorite tools to get our attention. Waiting exists only within the concept of time, and time is the very first thing he created, "in the beginning."[1] And ever since that beginning, God has worked within the wait.

When God sent his Son to be born into the world, four hundred years had passed since the people had heard a word from the Lord. It's difficult for me to wrap my mind around that much time, that much waiting. Not only had they not heard a word, but neither had their parents, their grandparents, or their great-grandparents. This was before readers could use Google and Bible Gateway to find answers, and they likely could not remember the last person in their family lineage who had heard a fresh word from the Lord. That feels pretty hopeless to me. I think I would stop believing—and stop waiting— if I couldn't even find the last person who had any real evidence of good news. That sounds like a perfect storm that would make me seriously prone to wander. I imagine I'd even begin to forget what it's like to hunger for his word.

In these four hundred years, God allowed a famine in the land. Not a famine of food, but indeed a famine of his word. In the silence, the people began to burn with a deep hunger for the sound of his voice. Sometimes God does that. He makes us wait so we can remember what we want the most.

After so many hundreds of years, the time came. *Came.* When Luke wrote the account of the birth of Jesus, he used that very phrase: "The time came for her baby to be born."[2] When the implications of this phrase jumped off the page at me, my perspective changed in a big way. Admittedly, when I am in a season of waiting, I can only seem to notice the passing of time in a negative way, like it's slipping through my fingers, and I can't stop it. The children are growing taller, the leaves are changing color, the clock is ticking, the sand is slipping through the hourglass. It's getting away from me. But Luke turned that whole perspective upside down. Time isn't merely passing. Quite the contrary, my friend. The Time is coming.

God wants to do something unique in my heart and in yours, and the process gives him fertile ground to do important work in our hearts, our relationships, and our very lives while we wait for the time to come. Waiting can be sacred space. It does not have to be passive or inactive. Actually, it can be filled with heartfelt anticipation and deep intention, and even sprinkled with joy.

The further you get from the beginning of the wait, the closer you are to what will become yours. A time is coming.

Your time is coming.

. . .

"How goes the new book?" Peter asks me one day in the car. It's a rather loaded question, since there is a fine tension between being interested in what I'm working on and holding me accountable to a deadline. I love interest, not pressure. Peter and I have been married for a couple of years now, but he still can't really know which way the pendulum is going to swing; it all depends on the day, the time I've spent writing that particular morning, and how I'm personally feeling about the work I'm doing. I suspect it's hard being married to a writer.

Sometimes he says, "How is the Wait?" and I mishear the homonym and think he asked about my *weight*, and things get a little dicey for a minute or two.

Or, since he knows I'm juggling this book and two others that I'm ghostwriting for other authors, he'll gently remind me to focus on my own words, saying, "Did you Wait today?" It's a gift to both of us when I can say yes.

"You know what? I've been thinking hard about some things," I offer. "I want to think about them with you." I start untangling the mess of my thoughts. I tell him how I've been pondering the process of waiting, and I believe that every season comes down to three stages: *Longing, Becoming,* and *Awakening.*[3]

"Tell me more about this," he says. I love those words. It's how he wooed my heart.

And so I tell him. There comes a point when you realize you are *separated* from something important to you— a person, a role, a goal, a longing, an achievement, a life stage. That's when the wait begins, and it brings an ache or a Longing. Maybe that's how we feel the silent sound of the clock ticking—in a deep, intuitive sense of longing.

Then, as you wait, you enter a stage of Becoming. Something is transformed—maybe it's your circumstances, or the details you can't manufacture on your own, or (my favorite) an actual change within you. Sometimes, the becoming is so slow that you can't feel the change. But in the waiting, you become something or someone new.

Finally, there is the Awakening, which is the moment when

you get what you waited for. You arrive at the moment you've longed for; you meet the goal. Sometimes the Awakening brings an acceptance that God is doing something entirely different from what you thought you wanted. Sometimes you get an awareness that you're content in this life you've been given, even without what you thought you needed. The Awakening is the sweet spot.

Waiting can seem so elusive, so hard to hold. That's what makes it miserable. But perhaps breaking it down into three stages makes it feel like there is a beginning, a middle, and an end. I've run it through my own gauntlet of examples, and so far, the formula has been foolproof.

Look at the caterpillar. She has this intuitive longing to grow into something different, so she separates from her social life with her caterpillar friends, and she makes her cocoon. She crawls inside to wait, and she slowly becomes a new and different creature. Finally, she breaks free in a moment of awakening, now with wings and wonder.

Jonah had a longing to do his own thing when he went in the opposite direction of Nineveh, so he created his own separation when he chose to disobey God. When he was swallowed by a big fish, Jonah began his three days of Becoming. He became open to direction, he became receptive to the voice of God, and, I imagine, he became covered in big-fish-stomach-grossness. When he was finally vomited onto the shore, Jonah awakened to dry land, the light of day, and a path to obedience.[4]

The Israelites left their home in Egypt, longing for

freedom, and they began a season of Becoming as they wandered through the desert for forty years. The people of Israel ambled for forty years before entering the Promised Land, though the technology of modern cartography tells us that they could have made the trip in just a few weeks, had God allowed them to know where they were going. The distance was not that far—a simple search on Google Maps shows it was a straight line of less than three hundred miles. Assuming they could travel a minimum of thirty miles per day, they could have made it in about ten days. Actually, that's a pretty ambitious pace for more than half a million[5] people to walk together, so let's slow them way down and consider all of the children, elderly, and camels. If they could only travel one mile per day, they still could have finished the journey in less than one year.[6]

In this case, let's not ignore the fact that their own choices played a role in the delay, since the consequence of their sin was that the first generation had to wander and wouldn't see the Promised Land. They made things worse with their own sin, and isn't that so often what we do too? Perhaps they could have finished the journey in less than a year, but *finishing* was not God's priority; the *waiting* was his priority. He was more interested in their obedience, their character, and the posture of their hearts. He was most interested in who they were *becoming*.

But not all of our waiting is the result of bad choices. Sometimes it's just the nature of how things go. I mean, I could even break down my morning routine into the stages:

the *longing* for a cup of coffee. I'm separated from my waking heart's desire. The goodness of modern technology turns the beans into grounds, and they *become* liquid gold in the coffee pot. With a splash of cream, the beverage is all mine, and an *awakening* happens on several glorious levels.

I talk to Peter's profile while he keeps his eyes on the road, and I save the *pièce de résistance* for last: "And it's even true of Jesus. When he died on the cross, he was separated from life, even separated from God. The disciples longed for their friend and leader. Mary longed for her son. Then his dead body was buried in the tomb, and the transformation began. Sometime in there, blood began flowing through his veins again, and he became healed, whole, and alive. And he emerged on the third day, just as he promised he would. The world awakened to hope."

I lay all of this before him, expecting him to be blown away by this discovery. I am even silent while he mulls it over.

But then he says, "I don't think it's true."

"What? You don't think *what's* true?"

"The becoming part."

"Why?"

"Well, I can think of sometimes when I had to wait, and nothing ever came of it. There was no healing, no transformation, no *becoming*. I was just angry because I was still waiting, and nothing changed."

I don't know what to say. I hadn't thought about that. In a few words, he has shattered my theory.

But, however reluctantly, I can see what he means. Peter

and I have each encountered different seasons of waiting, some of those on our own and some of them together. His waiting has been different from mine.

He says, "Not everyone is like you."

"How?"

"Not everyone is hopeful. Sometimes, waiting feels hopeless. It's not always neat and easy to sum up in three steps."

I consider this for a moment, partly defeated, partly curious. "So, what do you do in that place? What do you wish you had known when you've felt hopeless?"

"Well, I needed to do a lot more listening," he says. "I wish I had stopped arguing for what I wanted and instead listened to why I might not be getting it. I should have listened more, even just to the handful of people I trusted."

And then he says, "Look at me. I just realized something."

I look at him. He pulls my sunglasses down my nose.

"You don't have any eyebrows."

"I've never had eyebrows."

"I never noticed it before. You're like a hairless little mouse."

"True story." (Technically, I do have eyebrows. They're blonde and not worth mentioning. Or noticing, apparently.)

We started talking three years ago, and we haven't stopped. Our dialogue dances in and out of the heavy and real to the trivial and silly. From the transformation of Jesus in the tomb to the absence of hair above my eyes. And then back down deep again.

"I'd love to tell your story, if you'll let me," I say.

He pushes my sunglasses back into place.
"I'll think about that."

. . .

And so, here we are, you and me. All geared up to wait. I
chose the title of this book for three reasons. (And you know
I love a good list.) First, just you wait, because everyone takes
their turn in the waiting room. If you're waiting, it's because
we all do. It's your turn. I'm sorry about this long and painful fact of life, but shortcuts and microwaves don't work for
everything. Just. You. Wait.

Second, just you wait and see what God is doing. There
is so much happening underground, long before we see the
first bud break through the spring soil. And there is so much
happening within a new mom, long before she knows she is
pregnant. Before parents see a flickering white light on an
ultrasound screen, the baby has already begun to develop a
heart, brain, spinal cord, muscles, and bones. God is at work
behind the scenes, so many layers deep, in invisible ways you
cannot see . . . yet. Just. You. Wait.

Third, just you wait and see how ready you'll be if you
spend your waiting well. Waiting is not wasted time, but
rather a chance for you to study and prepare, to practice and
learn, to find a mentor and hone your skill. When your turn
comes after you've waited well, you can say, "Look out, world.
I am ready to shine. Just. You. Wait."

I have poured myself into these pages, asking God to join

me in the writing and to meet you on the page. Will you join me on the journey? As I love to say with each of my books: Let's write this together. The black parts are what I have to say, and the white space is for you and your thoughts. I don't know what your waiting looks like, but I do know that a person doesn't decide to read a book about waiting without feeling the realities of the battle with patience. Be gentle with yourself on this journey. You may even begin feeling excited about what God is going to do.

For many years now, my favorite conversations have unfolded when readers have stopped me in the grocery store, on the baseball field, at a bookstore, or at the airport to tell me about the journey we shared on the page. You've told me your stories of grief you thought would swallow you whole, of sadness that has torn you in half, of beauty from ashes and joy in the morning. You've shared with me the stories of your hard-won confidence, how you've learned to dance in the skin you're in, and how you've begun to like the person in your bathroom mirror. I look forward to the day when you will tell me about the journey in these pages, how we waited together for what God wanted to give you, what life had to show you, and the person you will become.

So buckle up, my friend. Waiting can be one wild ride.

Let's go.

PART ONE

Longing

"My name is Peter, and I'm an alcoholic."

I was sitting next to Peter in an Alcoholics Anonymous meeting the first time I heard him say these words. We were in a church basement, in a room with yellow walls, some holes in the carpet, a few posters with Bible verses, and the scent of freshly brewed coffee. "We drunks like our coffee," Peter says, raising his Styrofoam cup in solidarity. Cheers.

He had invited me to join him because it was his "fifth birthday." Five years of sobriety. It's a sacred celebration for an alcoholic, every time they pass a milestone and get a new chip. It's a much-deserved gold star. He invited me to meet his sponsor, to see a piece of the program at work, and to see the network of people who helped him get his life back. I was honored and humbled to meet this army of warriors battling a disease they are powerless against.

Peter first told me his story on our third date, over a morning brunch of pumpkin pancakes and breakfast tacos. He wanted me to know where he had been, what he had been through, and what he had once been all about, because he wanted to give me ample freedom to exit in case I decided it was all too much. He filleted his heart open with vulnerability and the full knowledge that I could choose to walk away from the mess. Little did he know, that level of honesty and transparency only made me feel safer. I'd far rather be with someone who knows his weaknesses than someone who thinks he doesn't have any.

A few months ago, I asked Peter to tell it to me again, his journey of waiting for freedom, as we sat in rocking chairs overlooking the rolling river in front of the deck of his family's cabin in the mountains. Might I say, private access to this sacred acreage is one of the perks of marrying into this family. My sons call it Peter's Forest, and they, too, are smitten with the whittling and the bonfires and the fishing and the tubing and the grasshoppers and the full moon and even the outhouses. This place has a fairy-tale quality that nurtures our souls. Here, suburban boys can become Tom Sawyer and Huck Finn, and a wife can carve a little space to ask her husband to revisit a difficult story.

"Honey, tell me the hardest thing you've had to wait for," I said.

"The hardest thing I've waited for . . ." Peter paused a moment. "Well, probably the hardest thing was waiting for my situation to change. That was a pretty hopeless walk through the desert, and it lasted a long, long time."

Peter got his first tastes of alcohol before he started high school. He got an early exposure to the ways it could change his personality, and it all seemed like a win-win at the beginning. He discovered he was funnier, louder, braver, and the life of any party. He carried this life skill into adulthood, sure that his affinity for alcohol was merely a preference, not an addiction. After all, he could stop if he wanted to, and it's not like he had to maintain a constant blood alcohol level. He didn't drink every day. But when it was time to party, he'd be sure to make it count. He'd start early and finish last. He knew how to hold his liquor and build his tolerance, and he liked that version of himself. Party Peter was a fun guy to be, and everybody else seemed to enjoy Party Peter too. Give him a few drinks, and your entertainment package was complete. He was a trained professional.

Peter got married and started his family in the late eighties, and there were a dozen good years of marriage with a woman he loved and a daughter and son he adored. But he brought alcohol into their family culture, and alcoholism makes a bad housemate. A whole lot of ingredients led to a great explosion, and after sixteen years of family life, he was a single man on his own. He was angry and bitter. He hated that he couldn't see his kids when he wanted, hated that he had to move, and hated that he had to work multiple jobs for money that would never be his. He'd earn enough to make ends meet, only to hand the check over for alimony, lawyers, and child support. The bar scene seemed more welcoming than ever, an acceptable alibi.

Peter said, "I wasn't the kind of guy who needed to keep alcohol in my blood all the time. But I was a binge drinker. It was difficult for me to ever be satisfied with one or two drinks. I needed many. My tolerance was built up so much that it took many drinks for me to feel the way I wanted to feel, which was happy, fun, and gregarious. But the thing about alcohol is that it's a depressant. *Happy, fun,* and *gregarious* can turn into *mean, angry,* and *belligerent* in the right circumstances. If I didn't get what I wanted, I'd get mean. Suddenly, a conversation would become a fight. I don't think it happened often, but that's the root of alcohol and the core of drinking. A belligerent drunk is unruly and cannot be reasoned with. With a few drinks, I could turn on a dime."

On his sober days, Peter would head out to a field where he talked to God and asked for a change. He'd walk the field and lament, "God, I feel ashamed. When can I get meaningful work? When can I pay off these debts? When can I be in a healthy relationship? Please, God. My children are ashamed of me. I can see it in their eyes. They don't want to come to my apartment and sleep on an air mattress, but it's all I have to give them. Please, God. Where are you?" He'd crack open another can from his faithful six-pack by his side, and he'd add, "Oh, and maybe I should cut back a little on my drinking . . . or maybe even quit. Maybe. That seems extreme, but if you could help with that, I'd appreciate it."

In 2011, things started to look up when he was cast in a TV commercial for the Colorado Rockies. If ever something deserved a couple of cold beers, it was an afternoon spent shooting a commercial for his favorite baseball team. He went to a bar to celebrate how fun the commercial had been, but that was just the pregame for a second event that night—this one with an open bar. As Peter says, "If they offered me an open bar, they were going to be on the losing end of that equation. Most of the time, at an all-you-can-eat situation, they'll serve heavy, glutenous foods. Breads, pastas—inexpensive foods that fill you up with one or two servings. But with alcohol, it's different. They had two bars at this place, one at each end of the ballroom. So, I'd make good friends with both bartenders, and then I'd strategically bounce back and forth between the two, timing it perfectly and never visiting so fast or so often that either one would notice how much I was drinking. Like I said, I was a trained professional."

Here's where it gets dicey. Peter left that open-bar party, and he drove himself home. He made it almost all the way there.

At the last stoplight before he arrived at his apartment complex, an officer stopped him. Peter wasn't slurring his words, but there was enough alcohol on his breath to prompt the officer to run his plates. The record showed that Peter had an outstanding ticket for a bar fight, and the terms of that ticket included that he wasn't allowed to drink for the next three months. The officer took him to the station, a Breathalyzer test showed he was over the legal limit, and Peter found himself in jail for the night. And he was none too happy about it. Livid is the better word, probably. He had almost gotten away with driving drunk *again*.

See, Peter hadn't intended to go to jail for this nonsense, he had a business presentation in the morning, and—most pressing on his mind—he had a new puppy at home. Sam was his black Labrador that he had rescued from a shelter, and they were just getting to know one another. They had finally managed to curb some of the anxiety Sam felt over being alone, and this night apart from Peter would be a set-back. Peter didn't want Sam to worry, and he wanted to call his sister to ask her to check on the dog. Harmless, right? Perhaps, but when you've broken the law and you've landed in jail, you're at the mercy of the officers. And the officers weren't concerned about the puppy's rough night.

The more they made him wait, the angrier Peter became because they had chosen not to do what he wanted. He could see them from his cell while they were watching the news and biding their time. Peter pressed the call button persistently and annoyingly, raising his own frustration and blood pressure, all to no avail. When someone finally came, the officer said, "We heard you say you were so angry."

"I'm very angry."

"We heard you say you were going to kill yourself because you're so mad."

"What? No, I never said that."

"Well, that's what I thought I heard you say, and we're going to need to protect you from yourself, sir."

When you're in jail, you're at the mercy of the officers. It's not wise to make them angry with your impatience.

They stripped off all his clothes, tied his naked body into a straitjacket from his neck to his knees, and locked him in solitary confinement for the night. Peter was in a small cell with a cold draft blowing across the cement floor he had to sleep on and a drain in the corner if he needed to use the bathroom. And so began the worst night of his life. Two Bible passages that he had memorized as a little boy came to mind: the Lord's Prayer and Psalm 23. He said them over and over to himself, waiting through a night of the deepest despair he had ever known.

Peter told me, "As for taking a man's dignity, that's as bad as it gets."

CHAPTER 1

The Wait You're In

Name the Longing

There have been seasons in my life when the waiting felt like it would be the end of me. When the waiting was a suffering all its own.

When my sons were five and three years old, their dad died very suddenly. Robb was sick for only twelve hours. The doctors thought he had the flu, and they sent us home from the ER with instructions to keep him hydrated on Gatorade and popsicles and settle in for the ten-to-fourteen days this bug would take to run its course. They said, "He won't die from this, but he will feel like he's going to."

They were only partly right. He had the flu, but those

symptoms masked a septic infection in his bloodstream that attacked his heart and lungs. He died in our home the next morning.

I was with him in his final moments, and I tried to save his life with chest compressions and mouth-to-mouth resuscitation on our bedroom floor, with screaming pleas begging him to stay alive. But his spirit slipped right through my fingers before the paramedics could arrive. He went from very healthy and completely with us to very sick and suddenly gone. He died just two days before Christmas. In a single hour one morning, everything changed. I became a thirty-one-year-old widowed single mom to two little boys who were fatherless and not yet in kindergarten. It felt and truly was as horrible as it sounds.

When other families were wrapping gifts and hanging their stockings on Christmas Eve, we were meeting with the funeral director for the final arrangements. I used words like *eulogy* and *cremation*. On Christmas morning, we each opened gifts that Robb had chosen and prepared, wrapped just a few days before, when everything still felt right in the world. The boys opened a battalion of army soldiers and remote-control cars from their daddy. I opened a pair of red satin pajamas, wrapped, tagged, and perfect.

That week between Christmas and New Year's is a foggy blend of images in my mind. We hosted Robb's wake and visitation hours at the coffee shop that was our favorite spot for a Friday-night date, and we had a memorial service at our church, appropriately ending with the Ohio State fight song.

My children and I were surrounded and held in every single way. In the weeks to come, as relatives and friends went home and everyone else went back to their lives, a thick darkness settled over me. I couldn't know it then, but I had entered a winter that would last for two years. Everything looked familiar, but nothing felt right. Robb didn't come home from work anymore.

Tucker, only five years old, became fiercely independent and determined to need nobody. He spilled milk as he poured it into cups, determined to get better fast at this big-brother role. He had lost one parent overnight, and he became compulsively aware that if I should die just as quickly, he might need to take care of himself and his brother at any time. Tyler, my baby at just three years old, controlled his world by refusing to change his clothes. Because when you're three years old, what you're wearing is the only thing you're in charge of. So, his wardrobe consisted of his Thomas the Train jammies or his Lightning McQueen T-shirt. My children each had their way of making sense of a loss too deep to explain.

My world got very small. I slept for two-thirds of every day, but the traumatic details of Robb's final moments played on a loop in my mind each time I drifted into any sleep that could bring rest. I didn't know how to see the path to the next day. I measured every victory in meals and moments and baths and bedtime stories. I saved a few ounces of energy for the end of the day, just to do something silly to make my children laugh, so they could know their mommy was still there, behind those layers of sadness. I waited and waited and waited for the depression to lift, for the sun to shine, for the winter to give way to spring.

In that devastating season of waiting, I learned that the unknown is the hardest part. I found myself wondering how long this would go on and just how much worse it all could get. But there was a strange comfort in the fact that, though my story was uniquely my own, I wasn't the only one who had walked this path of searing heartache. Others had felt invisible pain that seemed it could break them in two.

Certainly, when the apostle Paul wrote his letter to the church of Corinth, he was experiencing his own grief, uncertainty, and impatience, the sort of suffering ache we who have walked through dark seasons know all too well. I don't know the details of his pain, just like I don't know the excruciating nuances of yours. Still, his words comfort me. Because that's what the Bible does for me.

Paul wrote about his experience in Asia—

We were crushed and overwhelmed beyond our ability to endure, and we thought we would never live through it. In fact, we expected to die. But as a result, we stopped relying on ourselves and learned to rely only on God, who raises the dead.[1]

Yes. That. Everything that. I have a sign in my stairwell that says, "You never know how strong you are until you have no other choice." I'd like a second sign to say, much more importantly, "You never know what God can do until nobody else can do it."

. . .

Dear friend, as you are holding this book, please know this: You are very real to me. How I wish we could sit together over coffee in a couple of my favorite mugs. I'd ask you to tell me your story. What is happening in this season of your life? What are you waiting for?

Maybe you're single in a world that seems tailor-made for couples, and you're unspeakably tired of hearing the question "Why aren't you married yet?" at family reunions and Christmas dinners. The subtext of that question is actually "You look like a reasonably desirable person, so why hasn't someone snatched you up? You must have some hidden baggage or issues that only emerge when you're in a relationship long enough for those skeletons to step out. It's probably that. I mean, you look like someone who should be married, and yet you're not, so it's probably just that I can't see what's wrong with you." It's a terrible question without a real answer.

Maybe you're facing a health crisis. It's not going to kill you, but it's not going to go away either. You're going to have to live with it, and there seems to be nothing you can do to fix it. You can only manage the many symptoms.

Or maybe you're in a professional crisis. Maybe you planned to invest a lot of years in this line of work with this company, but now it seems you must make a change.

Someone has attacked your character with rumors about who you are and what you're about. Or there's a new boss in town and the new leadership structure is toxic and dangerous, and there seems to be nothing you can do about it. You thought there was a chance to advance, but as my friend Phil says, "The ladder you were climbing was leaning up against the wrong wall."

Maybe you're in a marriage that's not what it used to be, not what it's supposed to be, not what you want it to be. Neither of you wants a divorce, but the way you're living isn't working, and you feel like such a cliché. You didn't intend to become strangers sleeping in the same bed, but here you are. And there doesn't seem to be anything you can do to change it.

Perhaps you're in a parenting crisis. Maybe you have a child who's an absolute puzzle, or a child who's gone off the rails. You look at Facebook pictures of families with babies and small children, and you remember when you were in that life stage. You thought you could teach and train them enough in the early years to keep everything under control, but now you're wondering if any of your teaching landed anywhere at all. You miss the days when the hardest parenting challenges involved the cost of diapers and power struggles over fruit snacks.

Or maybe you're facing years of infertility. Your spouse doesn't want to adopt, and you can't afford fertility treatments; your options are few and your answers are fewer.

Maybe you're in a financial crisis. You're trying to "Dave

Ramsey" your way out of it, but every step in the right direction feels like a raindrop in the Grand Canyon. This isn't going to change—or get better—for a long, long time.

When I've been in any of these situations, I've begun to wonder if God is even aware of my plight. Is he paying attention? Is he listening? And if he's listening, why isn't he answering me? Why isn't he speaking? And most importantly, why isn't he *doing*? I've been tempted to think either he must be unaware or he doesn't care at all. I mean, let's be honest. Everybody's waiting for something. I must be pretty far down on his list.

I'm a firm believer in giving people the freedom to feel how they feel. Telling someone how to feel is like carrying a birthday cake into a gorilla cage: Everything is about to get messy, a fight will break out, and you're just asking to get your nose bitten off. I'm not about any of that. I promise not to tell you how to feel while you're waiting, and I won't rush you to a place of patience either. That's the whole thing about waiting: We can't change it. And the helplessness is what makes it so miserable.

I'm inviting you to name what you're waiting for, so we can keep it in front of us while we journey this path together. I'm in it with you. I'm so familiar with the ache of longing, and in this very moment, I'm still waiting on a good number of things. There's strength in numbers, and you're not alone. I believe we can do this. We can survive the wait with a handful of wildflowers named hope, courage, and laugh lines. Hear me on this: We don't have to like it. But we can learn a whole lot about who God is and what we're made of as we wade through the murky waters of waiting.

. . .

Somewhere, something incredible is waiting to be known.

SHARON BEGLEY

CHAPTER 2

The Great Waiters
Waiting Is a Big Deal to God

So here you are: waiting. Again. It's one of God's favorite tools to get our attention. In some ways, the Bible's title could be The Great Wait. The cast of characters could be the Great Waiters. (But that sounds a little like a dinner theater.)

Here's what I love most about the Great Waiters of the Bible: They were flawed. They were people just like us, trying to please God but often falling short. I mean, some of them got it. But most of them didn't. Which comforts me, since I usually don't either. The Great Waiters were no better at waiting than you and I are. Let's not kid ourselves: It's a universal weakness.

Adam waited for Eve, and there's so much about his long wait that I think we can't wrap our minds around. First of all, to be the first—and only—person on the planet. Theologians have invested decades in the debate over whether the seven days of creation are a literal time line or a poetic interpretation, but I'm not here to argue either side of that question. (It is, however, on the list of things I want to ask God about. I am also going to ask why he created mosquitoes, and why he decided that children's fingers should be exactly the same width as their nostrils.) Here's what we can read, though, in Genesis 2: Before God created Eve, he brought *all the animals* to Adam to see what he would call them, and Adam chose a name for each one. Adam waited long enough in his solitude to claim his role as the world's first zoologist, giving every single animal a name. That had to require some *time*. Adam had to encounter a whole lot of livestock, birds of the sky, and wild animals before he concluded there was no suitable partner for him.[1]

Noah waited a long time for the rain to even start sprinkling, all with his giant boat sitting on dry land where water had never (ever) fallen from the sky before. Then the storm began (and that first real storm on the earth was no little spring shower), the flood ensued, and there were the forty days and nights of rain—and that doesn't include the following months when he waited for the water to recede, for the ark to land on the mountaintop, and for the dove to bring back the olive branch.[2] Goodness. Noah's obedience was a long-term commitment to a downright strange project—and to patience.

And then there's Abraham's wife, Sarah—oh, my girl, Sarah. I just love her so much, specifically because of her impatience. She got so tired of waiting for a baby, so impatient waiting for the fulfillment of God's promises to her that she decided to take matters into her own hands. She thought she was too old to have a baby, and she concluded that God must have another woman in mind for the job, so she offered her servant for her husband to sleep with. The plan was that if the servant became pregnant and gave birth, Sarah would just take that child to raise as her own. (Apparently, transactions like this happened all the time.) How much I can relate to her, as I think of how often I've thought to myself, *I'll just help God along. Push his timetable a bit. He could clearly use my intervention, and I have a solid idea that absolutely could work. After all, people do things like this all the time.* But when it's not what God wants, nobody wins. Sarah just made everything harder for herself, not to mention the people around her. Hagar was put in a terrible position,[3] and Abraham turned into a man trying to placate the women in his life. That's a balancing act with a long list of ramifications.

Jonah is another one of my personal favorites on the list of people God loves. I mentioned him earlier, and it's because I have a special place in my heart for this guy. I see myself in him, too; he was fearful and proud. Jonah was quite capable of putting on a polished show of obedience, all while he was quietly—but stubbornly—resisting in his heart. He was an expert at being passive-aggressive. But God was more than willing to disrupt Jonah's comfort by putting him in the belly of a fish for three days and three nights. (Have you pictured how many rancid, smelly things he'd have found in that fish's belly with him? How long could *you* exist if the only place to lay your head was already slimy? God gave us imaginations for a reason; let's use them to our advantage when he is trying to teach us something.) Jonah's waiting is unique because its purpose was discipline. We don't have to assume that all seasons of waiting are about something we've done wrong, but—I confess it's true—more than once, God has put me in a notable time-out for an attitude adjustment. I get Jonah.

Even the parable of the Prodigal Son could also be titled "The Story of the Patient Dad." He waited, waited, waited with no visible sign of hope for such a very long time. At first glance, we might think the dad was passive, doing nothing to bring his son home. But in reality, the father was dealing with a human being with a will of his own. He couldn't make his son return to the goodness of the life waiting for him, so he waited for his son to come to his senses. He waited, ready to greet him and welcome him back home when the son was ready. The story says that "while [the son] was still a long way off, his father saw him coming. Filled with love and compassion, he ran to his son, embraced him, and kissed him."⁴ I love to picture that scene, as the father recognizes his son's silhouette, even from so far away. He knows that walk. I imagine he jumps to his feet and races down the path. He cannot get to his son fast enough. What a precious and long-awaited reunion.

Daniel waited through the night with a den full of lions. David waited in the cave. Moses waited forty years to be called by God. Abraham and Sarah waited twenty-five years for the arrival of their promised son, Isaac, and that was after waiting an entire lifetime to even get the promise in the first place. Joseph waited years in prison for a crime he didn't commit. Paul waited in prison. The early churches waited for their letters from him. And even Jesus waited thirty years to begin his ministry, though he was well equipped long before.[5] If God asked even Jesus to wait, why do I think he would speed up my process?

And oh, how I love Job. I mean, of all the heroes in the Bible, Job ranks in my top five favorites. I can't wait to have coffee with him someday. (I presume Job is a coffee drinker. It seems like he would have to be.) The way Job's story plays out in my mind, the whole thing starts with a meeting of angels before God. Everybody here? Everyone accounted for? Ah, wait. There is darkness in the room, the sneaky oppression of deceptive beauty.

"Where have you come from?" I imagine God saying. "This is a closed meeting, Satan. You're not invited to this executive board room."

And Satan says, "Oh, I've just come from roaming around the earth." That right there is the stuff horror films are made of: Satan and his minions trolling the earth, looking for trouble to cause, hearts to break, lives to destroy.

I want God to respond by saying, "Stay away from my kids, Satan. Back up. There's no room for you here, and you cannot take them from my hand, so don't even try." But he doesn't say that.

No, instead, God directs Satan's attention to one of his most faithful servants. I like to imagine God pulling out his wallet of family photos, letting the plastic frames unfold to the floor.

"Ah, there he is—there's Job. My goodness, he is among the finest. There's nobody like him! He is blameless, upright, obedient, and he certainly runs away from you, Satan."

"Ha!" Satan replies. "You bought his favor! You're like the long-distance grandparent who spoils his favorite grandchild. Who wouldn't love you with all of those benefits you've lavished on him? A house, a successful livestock business, family, money—I would be willing to bet that if you take away everything he has, he won't be quite so faithful to you. I believe he would curse you to your face."

"Very well," God says. "He is yours. Give it your best shot."

Satan is set free on a path of destruction, and nobody can destroy quite as thoroughly as the prince of evil. Sure enough, he takes everything that belongs to Job. Everything.

Take a moment to consider the extremes of Job's pain. His family is dead, his money is gone, his possessions have vanished, and then he comes down with a skin disease that probably drives him nearly mad with itching and pain. Picture this happening to *you*. How would you respond to God? Who could blame you for cursing God as you're dying?

But all of Satan's best efforts don't work. He can't get Job to curse the name of God, but still he doesn't give up trying.

Satan negotiates with God repeatedly, asking him to change the rules. He wants to cause even greater pain, loss, questions, and doubt in Job's life. He's out for blood, literally.

Side note: My compliments and appreciation to Job's friends, who—for one week—sit quietly with their friend. They cry with him, sit with him, and don't say a word. But then wisdom seems to elude them. They open their mouths, and everything changes.

Having been in a place of utter desolation, I need to tell you one of the most gracious gifts you can give to someone in their darkest hour: your sympathy, companionship, presence, and silence. Don't talk; just be.

Yes, waiting creates an ache. But there are degrees to that ache, a spectrum of patience required. Waiting for the barista to call your name and announce your drink is far different from waiting for the doctor to call with the test results. Waiting to go into labor is far different from waiting to see the face of the baby who died before she was born. Waiting for relatives to arrive for Christmas break is far different from waiting to see someone who has died, someone who is gone from this earth forever. There are some waits that don't end on this side of heaven, and we must be patient with ourselves—and with others—who are waiting for something this world cannot provide. Don't try to fix it. Just be with them.

I think the verses in Job 19 are some of the most important in the entire book. Job is taking the heat from Satan and the unwarranted advice from his friends.

Job says,

Oh, that my words could be recorded.
    Oh, that they could be inscribed on a monument,
carved with an iron chisel and filled with lead,
    engraved forever in the rock.

But as for me, I know that my Redeemer lives,
    and he will stand upon the earth at last.
And after my body has decayed,
    yet in my body I will see God!
I will see him for myself.
    Yes, I will see him with my own eyes.
I am overwhelmed at the thought![6]

Basically, he tells his friends, "Listen, guys, I wish there were some way to write down my words so you could see them and never forget them. I want them written down forever, even as tattoos on your hands. Hear me well: When this is all over with, you'll see—and I will, too—that my God is real, he is here, and he has loved me all this time. He will rescue me. I cannot wait another day, but I will. Because I know that I know."

I read those words, and I want to raise my coffee cup to Job right now. Yes, Job. I hear you. I know that my Redeemer lives, and someday I will see him. I—and everyone else—will see that he is real, he is here, and he has loved me all this time. Sometimes the wait is so painful, it breaks my heart all over again. I cannot wait another day, but even on the hardest of days and the darkest of sunrises, I will wait another day. Because I know that I know.

I choose to trust that I will someday see what I have been waiting for all this time.

. . .

We can know that God is the same yesterday, today, and tomorrow, and he doesn't play favorites. So how he leads other people will explain how he leads us as well. It's why Bible stories matter. If you want to learn about the nature and character of God, then you can read stories of God's interactions with his people to see examples of how he wants us to live.

What do the stories of the Great Waiters show me about waiting? What did they do while they waited?

While Adam waited for Eve, he explored the Garden, named the animals, and learned how to be a human being.

While Noah waited for the rain, he got busy with what he had: a lot of wood and some specific measurements.

While the father of the Prodigal Son waited for his boy to come home, he kept his eyes on the horizon, waiting for good news.

While Daniel waited, he remained faithful in prayer and firm in his convictions. He didn't change his mind, even when compromise would have made more than a few things easier for him and his friends.

While Joseph waited in prison, he didn't waste his energy on the question *Why?* (Though I imagine he asked that word, he didn't let it drain him with dead ends and nonanswers.) Instead, he focused his sights on answering *What should I do now?* He did his best with each small task given to him, and he stayed close to God. As his situation began to turn around, he was ready for every opportunity because he had not wasted his time.

While Job waited for answers, he felt how he felt. He asked honest questions in the face of his darkest hours.

While David waited in the cave, he wrote poems and songs.[7]

While Paul waited in prison, he wrote letters.

And while Jesus waited for permission from his Father to begin the ministry he was sent to do, he spent every single day loving the people in front of him.

Here's what I see in all of those stories: There is always work to be done in the waiting. Sometimes the work is hands-on and physical, and other times it is a solitary journey of soul-searching. Sometimes the work is a discipline of noticing, a practice of being alert and aware; sometimes it is about being patient, loving, and present. But when we choose to surrender to the moment, when we seek to believe this moment is part of a larger story, and when we embrace the ache of the longing, the wait is never wasted.

The Lord enters the journey of those who wait. He shows himself.

. . .

Take courage, my heart, stay steadfast, my soul
He's in the waiting.

"TAKE COURAGE," BETHEL MUSIC

Wait for the LORD;
* be strong and take heart*
* and wait for the LORD.*

PSALM 27:14, NIV

CHAPTER 3

Ridiculous Waiting

In Line at the DMV

I'm not especially great about such things as renewing a driver's license. I can't worry about everything, and this particularly worrisome errand falls into the "Other" category. When Robb and I moved to Colorado, I got my first speeding ticket well over a year after we had become residents. The police officer stood at my driver's-side window, holding my Ohio license in his hand, and asked, "Have you recently moved here?"

"Just a few weeks ago," I said.

"How many weeks ago?"

"Well, it's been probably, maybe, like, fifty-four."

When I got that new Colorado license, as the officer so

strongly urged me to do, I remember thinking, *My word, this thing expires in ten years. I'll be what, like,* thirty-five years old? *I wonder if we'll have any kids. I wonder if I'll look anything like this picture anymore.*

Yes, yes, and yes, young lady. You'll just be a deeper, stronger version of the girl in that mug shot. And you can't possibly imagine how different your life will be.

When Peter and I got married, I decided I wanted to take his last name as my own. A legal name change meant that I was again at the mercy of the Department of Motor Vehicles. I marked the calendar for my official Name-Changing Day, which is different from a Wedding Day and also different from Marriage-License Day. It turns out that updating your name and relationship status on Facebook doesn't count as making actual, legal changes. You must really want to change your name. These things don't just happen.

I would devote one whole day to navigating the legal documents. I reserved some hours in the morning to get after this task, and I was wholly committed to refusing stress and negativity. I resolved that I would be peaceful and joyful, and I would lean into as many of these four hours as necessary to make my way down the Candy Land path to getting my name changed.

Scratch that. It's not Candy Land. It's Chutes and Ladders.

I started with the Social Security Office, where I changed my name, and then I headed to the DMV to get the corresponding photo on a new license. I began most logically with the DMV office closest to my home, which is, of course, one that doesn't issue driver's licenses. Deep breath. This would not be a problem for me, no sir, since I was not doing stress and negativity. Off to the DMV that's twenty minutes south. Good thing I had a list of good podcasts to keep me company in the car.

I checked in at the kiosk at the DMV. I was number 260, and they were presently on number 231. *Good thing I'm not doing stress and negativity today*, I thought. *I even brought a book. Because of course I did.* I had just opened a book when I heard an omniscient voice over the loudspeaker. "Customer #260, please come to Suite 143, Counter D2."

Wait. I think that's me. What room am I in? More importantly, is this a suite? Are any of these really suites? Let's be honest with ourselves, DMV. I mean, really.

Using my skills of deduction and map reading that I learned in second grade, I deduced that I was in "Suite" 141, and I saw that 143 was across the hall. As I walked the seven steps across the hall, the omniscient voice repeated herself: "Customer #260, please come to Suite 143, Counter D2."

Right. Got it. Here I am. On my way.

There was one person at the counter, so I took a seat in the row of orange plastic chairs. When she finished, I expected them to call me up next. That's because I am a rational human being who thinks logically. But the employee behind the counter addressed something insanely important at her computer screen instead. Type, type, type.

I was the only person sitting in this "suite." Silently. She typed. Type, type, type.

But I wasn't doing stress and negativity, remember? So this was no problem. I would wait.

Type, type, type. Maybe forty-five seconds passed. Then she said, "Ma'am, what's your number?"

"Two-sixty."

She looked at the screen. "I deleted your number." Type, type, type.

"What? Why?"

"Because I called it twice."

"I came as soon as I heard you."

"Well, I called you twice."

"And I came immediately."

"Not the first time." Type, type, type.

"Ma'am, you called me the first time less than two minutes ago, and I've been sitting here for one and a half of those minutes."

Type, type, type. This is how and why sloths are cast as DMV employees in animated films. Because stereotypes are legitimate.

I am not doing stress or negativity today, I reminded myself. *And it's a* good thing.

"Ma'am," I ventured, "I'm here right now." I wanted to add, *in front of you, as a living human being. And, by the way, I choose to believe you are a human being as well. Maybe we could be human beings together, even though you had to call me twice.*

Type, type, type.

"Fine." She sighed. "Number 260." At which point I stepped forward. She didn't even have to tell me twice.

And that's when I learned that the Social Security Department needs twenty-four to forty-eight hours to change a name in the system, so consider this your public service announcement: If you take one day off work to change your name, it will not be enough days.

So, two days later, I returned to my favorite place. This time, I brought my mom, since it's always a good idea to bring a friend along for moral support for invasive procedures. She happened to need a new license as well, so we took our numbers: 474 and 475, respectively.

Let me tell you what I learned on this second visit: Women get *dolled up* for the DMV. We all know this picture will be our standard ID for the next decade or so. And in all honesty, I had delayed the errand more than once because I hadn't washed my hair that day and I didn't want to go on record looking greasy. But I'm not kidding you—there was one girl there dressed to the nines, all the way down to her shoes. She really could have been on her way to Homecoming. Or at least a casual prom.

As we waited in those orange plastic chairs, I heard a clerk ask someone, "And how much do you weigh today?"

I gasped. Audibly. What is this? *The Biggest Loser*? Am I going to have to step onto some giant scale in my underwear and watch the numbers tease us all as they bounce from 294, 123, 405, 79 . . . until it makes a giant and public declaration? Because this scene is going nowhere good. I was more nervous to take my spot in line than I've been in any dentist's waiting room. And I knew I certainly couldn't make the clerk have to call me *twice*.

There she sat behind the counter, asking *each and every* person, "And how much do you weigh today?"

One woman whispered, "Um, one-fifty-five."

And the clerk responded in full voice, "I'm sorry, did you say one-five-five or one-six-five?" Good grief! Are you *kidding me*??

I thought maybe I would slip her a note with three numbers on it, and I'd let her order them to her liking. Just please don't make me say this nonsense out loud.

When my mom took her turn, the clerk said, "Ma'am, should we go ahead and list your hair as 'white' and not 'brown'?"

"Well, yes. Yes, I suppose we should."

"I see your license expires in ten years, so do you want to go ahead and list your next of kin?" Maybe we could go ahead and call it an emergency contact—since it's a *driver's license* and not a *living will*. Shall we?

"And ma'am, do you wear contact lenses?" she asked my mom.

"I do."

She looked up, frankly a little bit surprised. "You do? And do you have them in right now?"

"I do."

She beamed and *patted my mom on the hand*, like you might affirm a very elderly senior citizen for taking a stroll down the hall with her walker. "Oh! Good for you!" she said.

When it was my turn, she breezed through the same set of questions with me, once we got past that pesky weight issue. My hair color is the same; my eyes are the same; yes, I'll be an organ donor. And then she said, "Do you want to go ahead and keep the same emergency contact you have on file?"

(Apparently, they call it your "emergency contact" when you're under the age of forty.)

"Actually, is it Robb Williford?"

"Oh, I don't know. It doesn't show up on the screen. I can either keep it the same or change it."

"I'm sure it's Robb"—and here's where I always wish I could think of a different way to say this—"but he died a few years ago."

"Oh. So, do you want to list someone else? Just in case?"

Just in case . . . what? Just in case Robb is perhaps not still taking emergency phone calls? Yes, I want to list someone else. Let's go with the new husband.

In all fairness, she did take a moment to then step out of the questioning protocol and acknowledge what I had just said. And that's when I found myself standing at the DMV counter talking about Streptococcus pneumonia and why people need spleens and how fast sepsis takes over and how young I was—and am—and how many kids I have and how resilient they are. (I think she's going to buy a book.)

She looked back at my mom. "Now, ma'am, this license is good for five years, and that's true for everyone. So it's not about your age or anything."

(Thank you for clarifying.)

"And you can renew it in two years," she added.

"Two years? Didn't you just say it's good for five?"

"Yes."

"So I can renew it in two years but it expires in five?"

"Yes."

"I'm sorry," my mom said. "There's something about this math that I'm not understanding. But maybe I'll renew it four times in the next eight years and then it will be good for twenty years." That's right, ladies and gentlemen: She's still got her quick wit, despite the white hair and next of kin.

The whole thing was befuddling. Seriously. (If you're wondering how long the license is valid and why there are multiple indicators in this conversation, then you're in good company.)

And then, as if all of this weren't just crazy upon crazy, I signed my name wrong. And they only give you one try in that little box, you know. So now, for the rest of time, I—the girl who is meticulous about her handwriting on a score sheet to a card game—will have to carry around a driver's license with a jacked-up *H*.

When my driver's license arrived in the mail, Tuck took one look at it and said, "Huh. Well, at least it actually looks like you." As opposed to the last one, apparently.

Dear twenty-five-year-old Tricia, forget what I said about looking relatively the same in ten years. Also, you will have two kids whom you can count on for all kinds of honesty and affirmation.

Ridiculous waiting is the most trying on my patience, and I believe that's because it seems especially unnecessary. But patience is like a muscle: It gets stronger when you use it, and it becomes more versatile when you stretch it. Patience in ridiculous waiting can make you far better at the waiting that actually makes sense.

Anyway, all of that to say, if you need to practice ridiculous waiting, the DMV is your place.

Make an appointment. And pack some snacks.

You're welcome.

. . .

Waiting is one of the great arts.
MARGERY ALLINGHAM

CHAPTER 4

Longing to Begin

Waiting to Create

I am an absolute junkie for learning, and I get a dopamine rush from intelligent conversations. Add in sharp listening skills and a conversational quick wit, and I am toast. It's all I really want in life. So when I was invited to a writer's retreat recently, an incubated three days in a think tank with writers, authors, editors, and influencers, it was everything I wanted and needed that I didn't know was missing in my life. I acquired pages and pages of notes and ideas and conversations over hours and wine and appetizers with new friends. Bekah was my roommate, and she's a darling firecracker in a little tiny frame full of big ideas. She had released her first book earlier that year, a book about her life on the move as a military wife. She writes flawless prose that reads easy and poetic, and then, all of a sudden, she punches me in the face with humor. I love her writing. Bekah had a three-year-old girl, a one-year-old boy, and a baby on the way. (Kudos to the girl who released a book in the middle of *that* season.) Now she found herself in the aftermath of her book release, trying to figure out how and when to write the next book, and what creativity can look like in those years of preschool and naps and potty training.

Now, there are some who would say, "This isn't her season for writing. She should slow down and be where she is." And there are some women who can slow down and be where they are, who can delay their big ideas until the speed limits are lifted and the season opens like a highway. But some of us can be really good moms while we have a lot of ideas brewing on the stove-top. Some of us can only read *Goodnight Moon* one more time if we've spent some solid time reading other books with big words and bigger ideas. When you tell a young mom to stop doing what she loves because all she may do is take care of those she loves, I fear you make her heart less available to the very people she loves most. We all need space to grow, especially those of us who are in a season where we are wearing other people's bodily fluids.

Bekah is in that place that I remember so well. She's in the throes of the dichotomy of loving her children so much that it hurts, of loving the role but hating the tasks, of wanting to be with them but dying for a break, of daily tasks that never stay finished, of I-Love-You-But-Please-Stop-Touching-Me. She's in the tension of knowing it passes so quickly, coupled with the greater awareness that this day is so *unbelievably l-o-n-g.*

I confessed to her about the day that I remember saying to my children, "Did you know that Mommy is smart?" It wasn't my finest hour, that day when I felt like I had to defend my college degree to my three-year-old. I wanted that season with them, but I also wanted more and bigger. My mind swirled with the more and the bigger. It's hard, that season of so constantly belonging to people who need so endlessly.

When my children were toddlers, I decided that maybe I could think of myself as a missionary to a foreign land. This season called for loving the natives, learning their language, feeding them before they grew restless and agitated, and occasionally negotiating with terrorists. When my youngest started kindergarten, I felt like I had crossed the biggest finish line of my life thus far: three hours to myself per day. Welcome, furlough.

Have you ever felt God calling you to something, but you feel like you're stuck in neutral? You may feel the seed of something big and important, the ideas mounting and the dreams growing, but maybe you're in a season of waiting, traveling at a pace that won't let you get to work just yet, or at least not as fast as you planned to.

Your life is the making of a grand story, the stuff of a great adventure. But it may not feel that way when you're emptying the dishwasher (again) or taking the dog to the vet (again) or cleaning out the backseat from the trash and nonsense your kids left behind (again). (Speaking hypothetically, of course.) But it really is.

In the mess and the mundane, in the redundancy of tasks that never stay finished, you are a living, breathing miracle. We are each on a long journey home, but we have no idea how long this trip will take. We have been assigned tasks for which we feel unprepared and ill-equipped, we've been called to wait in lines and seasons that are longer than we feel is necessary, and this calls for strength we do not have. We are called to walk down dark paths that are poorly lit. Or most challenging, to simply be still while we feel the world is moving on without us.

(Perhaps you are reading this from the other side of Contentment Avenue. Maybe you are a mom who has absolutely found yourself in the best parts of this role, and these paragraphs feel unrelatable to you because this impatience is exactly the opposite of how you're feeling. Girl, I'm so happy for you. Anytime someone delights in their season of life, I want to raise my glass and pour another. Let's open our hearts and minds big enough to hold both ends of the spectrum. Just like God makes each child differently, he has created each mom differently too. We are allowed to stop judging the moms who are good at Halloween costumes, just like we are allowed to delight in the ones who are good at managing an office. We so deeply long for respect *from* each other, so let's be willing to offer respect *to* each other.)

When you're in that place of dancing between the now and later, you can do one of two things: You can do everything in your power to get started, or you can wait until you have specific instructions to move forward. And here's the beauty: You can find your own place on that spectrum, your own measure of ingredients. There is wisdom in taking the steps you can take now, and there is wisdom in waiting to know which steps to take.

I remember when I was pregnant for the first time, getting ready to have my baby. I felt like there was a ticking clock, like I had to get all the learning done before someone placed this baby in my arms. I understood that not only would they let me take him home, but they would *expect* me to. But parenting is a lifetime class, not a crash course for three trimesters. Most moms-to-be don't spend our entire pregnancy quizzing every pediatrician we know, taking classes on how to make our own baby food, buying out all the diapers in the tri-county area, and practicing Lamaze breaths day in and day out. But neither do we just sit and wait for the baby to be born. No, we take intentional and deliberate steps in anticipation of bringing this child into the world, into our family, and into our home. We buy maternity clothes. We stock up on onesies and burp cloths. We drink a lot of water. We read books, and we talk to moms who have given birth, adopted, recovered from C-sections, breastfed, bottle-fed, sleep-trained, and coslept. We may tour the maternity ward at the hospital and interview a pediatrician. But we don't do it all in one day, and we can't do it all at one time.

Here's something I've always been abundantly thankful for: As new moms prepare to bring the baby home from the hospital, they don't have to read books on parenting teenagers. The good news is that a newborn comes to you with very basic needs that you can meet. They don't come home needing consequences and curfews and your Wi-Fi password.

You don't have to know everything in order to get ready for the next thing.

You can take natural, commonsense steps that align with your passions, interests, and God's calling on your life, so you can be ready when he gives you your opportunity. He will show you the way, either by opening doors or closing them. He will bring to you the resources, network, and mentors you need. He may call you to do a brand-new thing, and he may call you to do exactly what you already know how to do. He may even give you a dose of both.

Noah could teach us a thing or two about this tension between waiting and starting. Think about the enormity of the task, of all that he was asked to do in preparation for the world's greatest downpour, all without evidence of even a cloud in the sky. And then all those animals! I've read recent studies that estimate that the total kinds of animals on the boat were about 1,500, and pairs of every kind joined Noah and his family in the boat—including seven pairs of every kind of animal used for sacrifice. The "worst-case scenario" estimates that Noah may have cared for as many as 7,000 animals.[1] If I were Noah, that would have stopped me in my tracks. On a number of levels. (The poop factor alone is staggering. But let's not digress.)

I know myself fairly well, and I know that on God's

instructions, I would have been like, "Right, so, I've got this blueprint for a boat, and that's going to take me a few years for starters, but then what? All these animals? How in the world will I manage that? I can't imagine tracking down all those animals, so I better not even start a project I can't finish."

But Noah is a better person than I am, which doesn't come as a shock to any of us. He got right to work when God told him to build the ark, and he did everything exactly as God asked him to do it. Meanwhile, all of creation followed God's instructions as well, and each kind found their way to Noah and his ark. All the little husband-and-wife bunnies, snakes, donkeys, lions, tigers, and bears. Did you know that God brought all the animals to Noah? Maybe I missed that day of Sunday school, or maybe it just never occurred to me to connect those dots, but I guess I missed that nugget of information along the way. I guess I always thought that Noah sent his sons all over the known world for the Great Animal Kingdom Roundup. But I just found this detail, and I love everything about it.

So often, I do just the opposite of Noah. I worry about details down the road, when (a) I have no control over them, and (b) that is not what's in front of me to do right now. Plenty of tasks are sitting right in front of me, and I can start there. Noah had measurements and wood, and he got started. He didn't get all agitated over what would happen later; he just got to work now. I can't help but believe his head was spinning with questions even as he built a giant ship in his backyard. But he kept hammering as he thought.

If God has asked you to do something, get started. Don't neglect your calling for today because you don't have a plan for when it gets bigger than you. And don't neglect the task because you don't know how you'll ever have time to finish it in this season you're in. Don't worry yet about how you'll write the book or sell the tickets or promote the business or finish well. When it's time, God will bring you what you need so you can do what he's asked you to do. He brought together the entire animal kingdom for a year-long cruise, didn't he? Surely what you need is less daunting than that.

Here is a little spoonful of encouragement to those of us who are weary of waiting to even get started: You don't have to wait one more minute to start learning what you're longing to learn. Perhaps you can get started by simply finding someone to learn from.

Sometimes I think we've gotten the definition of mentoring a little bit wrong. Especially in the church world, we tend to think mentoring calls for a formal ask, a commitment of many weeks, a book to study, and a curriculum to follow. We tell ourselves and each other that we can't step into a mentorship without a clear plan followed by weeks of fasting and discernment. I mean, all those things *can* be true, sure. But that kind of analysis and preparedness can also suffocate a friendship or cause a decision to be nearly unmakeable. It can paralyze the process and keep us from beginning.

But really, you're allowed to learn from anyone you want to, and finding a mentor is easy. You can ask her. Or him.

Just straight up ask. When you invite someone to teach you what they know, you've found a mentor.

Each generation is meant to train the next generation, not pattern them in their own image. Even when Paul instructed his readers to imitate him,[2] he didn't mean they should literally mimic him. He was inviting them to watch and model his character and his godliness as he chased after the model of Jesus Christ. He was inviting them to study and learn on their own, and he was offering himself as a mentor.

A mentor can teach you quite a bit over one cup of coffee, all without a long-term commitment. And let's not forget about the power and possibilities of being mentored by someone you've never met, or you will likely never meet. Books, podcasts, and online learning make it possible for us to metaphorically brush elbows with the heroes in our field. In this season of waiting for your big break, you can study and learn from the people who seem to be where you want to be, doing what you want to do. You may feel sidelined, but you are not powerless as you wait.

So I said to Bekah, my writing friend in the throes of the most demanding years of parenting, "Here's what you have to know: You will never, ever have less time to yourself than you have right now. You're trying to do many things for many people you love, to love them well but not lose yourself. In this season, every accomplishment is a victory. *Everything*. Everything they do, everything you do, and definitely anything you do in the name of finding your writing voice. Celebrate anything, and reward yourself extravagantly and often. Life will get easier in some ways, more difficult in others, but later, your children will be busy with their own lives. Right now, you are their life. Take heart, young mom, fellow missionary who feels like you're navigating a foreign wilderness you've somehow created. There are so many long miles between the really gratifying moments. Sometimes finding margin is the very hardest part.

"Take a step to begin what you've been called to do. And please, celebrate everything you can think of."

. . .

I will prepare, and someday, my chance will come.
ATTRIBUTED TO ABRAHAM LINCOLN

Don't tell me not to fly,
I've simply got to.
"DON'T RAIN ON MY PARADE," BOB MERRILL AND JULE STYNE

CHAPTER 5

Where Is the Sunshine?
Waiting to Heal

Grams was the kind of grandma who kept her cookie cupboard stocked with each grandchild's favorite cookie, and in the bathroom cabinet, she kept eight toothbrushes, each one with a name on it. Grams had no time for poor dental hygiene, nor could she tolerate a day without a cookie. A day without dessert is like a night without stars.

Grams taught me that life is uncertain, and sometimes you should eat dessert first. She took us out for dinner quite a bit, for pizza or spaghetti or hamburgers, and when the server came to ask if we had left any room for dessert, she would be woefully and dramatically disappointed that there wasn't room. Oh, how we longed for room! Grams said, "Someday, we will come here and eat dessert first. And after the ice cream, if there's still room, *then* we'll have our dinner." Every once in a while, she followed through with that grand plan. Giant ice-cream sundaes, followed by vegetables and a main dish (but only if there was room).

Grams taught me that it's better to enjoy your company while they're in your home than to leave the party to do the dishes. Dishes will be there later, long after the guests are gone. Don't mistake the pressing task for the fleeting joy.

She taught me to love books. And it wasn't until I was grown that I learned that she didn't like to read. She didn't like it, but she wanted me to love it. So she read to me, one afternoon after another.

She taught me the value of getting your work done in the morning so you can play all afternoon. She intercepted my parents to tell them they should let me go to prom with the (much older) young man who had asked me. (I guess I've always had a thing for older men, come to think of it.)

She taught me the beauty of hello and good-bye. The first moments together determine the mood for the rest of the day, so greet your guests—and your husband—at the door. And good-byes matter, so finish well. Walk your husband to the door, and walk your guests to the car. Send them off with the fragrance of you and your love. She taught me to put an onion in a little melted butter on the stove if your husband comes home before you have a dinner plan. If it smells like something is cooking, he will be far more patient. She taught me that if you buy something for your husband while you're shopping, he won't care how much you spent on your other purchases. She taught me to never underestimate how much my husband loves me, but to never overestimate the power of another woman's attention or affection for him. Bottom line: Stay pretty and interesting and interested.

Grams taught me the heroic practice of doing the next thing in front of you. She walked through many dark seasons, and she seemed so heroic on that side of life's journey. But she didn't feel heroic. She had simply, only, and always done the next thing life handed her to do. She sent a husband off to war. She cared for many loved ones to their dying breaths, walking them to the last second of this life. She broke a hip and faced multiple surgeries to reconstruct it. Her husband died at home in her arms, the man who was her soul's companion and the greatest laughter of her life. And as she faced her own daunting diagnosis of Parkinson's disease, she did the next thing, one day after another, right until the day the dementia stole her mind. Grams simply, only, always did the next thing.

Grams was smart and wonderful. So when the hospice center called to say she had only a few days to live, that she had entered the stage of "actively dying," I packed up my two toddlers and I went to Ohio. If death was imminent, then I wanted to be near.

We rushed to her side. We said our good-byes. And then she didn't die. One day after another came and went, and Grams stayed . . . for more than two weeks. I began to wonder if I should go back home, but I feared she would die, and I'd have to get back on a plane to return because I couldn't bear to miss her memorial service. (It didn't help that Robb was at home in Colorado, pining for me and a home-cooked meal. For all that Grams had taught me about how to love a husband well, I shelved it all for her final days. He was healthy and strong and smart, and he could heat up his own dinner, for crying out loud.) So I stayed. And so did she.

Grams' dying days were long ones. And unlike the quick thief of Robb's life a few years later, which I didn't see coming and could not prepare for, Grams' final days gave me time to wait and watch. Waiting gives you time to watch.

I watched Grams come face-to-face with death, all without fear. And I learned this: We all have to face death. Everyone dies. Nobody gets out of here alive. Even the people who exercise and take their vitamins and eat green and drink organic. Everyone has an expiration date. In the end, there's an end.

But I also saw this: We don't have to face it alone. Doctors may treat, nurses may nurture, and family may even be so fortunate to sit with you to the very end. But only God can carry you across the threshold and safely home. Don't face death without God. Don't even talk about death without talking to God. He's the only one who can guide you through the valley and safely home, and he promises that he will. Jesus said, "I will come back and take you to be with me."[1] He doesn't delegate that task to anyone else. He takes full responsibility, and he reserves that job for himself. So as we waited for Grams to go, we were actually waiting for Jesus to decide to take her. He wouldn't abandon her in the moment of death.

After fifteen days of waiting, Grams breathed her final

breath here. She slipped away from us, finally, leaving behind the pain and the white hair and the memories and the legacy. And all her grandchildren went to lunch together on that day. After all those weeks of waiting, we finally laughed together once again. Not because we didn't miss her, but because we missed her very much. In her honor, we ate dessert first.

. . .

When death comes at the end of a long life, we don't wonder if it was time. We don't wonder if God is good. But when death comes unexpectedly to a child or a teenager or a young parent, it is hard to believe that death can be a good thing. It is hard to believe that God is a good God.

Maybe you are in that dark valley now, the valley of questions. Maybe the fingers that turn this page are the same that felt a fevered brow turn cold as illness gave over to the death of someone you loved very, very much. Maybe the eyes that read this sentence have also learned the very color of death on the face of a parent, friend, husband, wife, or child. Maybe you are in the dark and cold shadow of endless loss, in the long night of waiting for morning's joy to come again.

Can we talk about that kind of wait? It's a journey unlike any other. It calls for a patience all its own, that waiting and watching for signs of spring. The grief journey is a hard path to walk. Yes, it's difficult because it's long and dark and winding, but it's also hard because not everyone understands your sadness. They did at the beginning. They understood at the funeral. They understood at the graveside, while the soil was fresh and dark at the cemetery. But very soon, they no longer understood. Or maybe they didn't have the capacity to understand. They returned to their routines and calendars and appointments and lives. They meant to understand longer, sure. But they couldn't stick around the way grief could. Grief has some serious staying power.

Why does grief linger the way it does? Why does sorrow remain so long? What gives it this lasting strength? Why can't sadness just do its thing and then leave you alone?

It stays because you are dealing with far more than one emotion. You are dealing with the loss of far more than a person. The memories alone are a tidal wave. You're not just dealing with sadness. You're dealing with disappointment and abandonment and anger. Anger at life. Anger at death. Anger at the diagnosis or the accident or the situation that took the person you love. You may feel anger at the person who died, maybe for their carelessness or selfishness, or for their inability to get well, or for how they left you behind for a much better place. You may feel anger at God, and your anger may live hard and strong in the word *why*. Emotions are not right or wrong; they just are. Further, emotions are not time-bound. It's not true that time heals all wounds; *healing* heals all wounds. In the face of grief, we may not even know all the things we're mad about, and we don't have to place extra guilt on ourselves for not healing fast enough. Emotions exist outside of time, and sometimes they live outside the bounds of logical explanation. You just feel how you feel.

In my imagination, memories are tangible things we collect and store. And I like to imagine that we carry them in a box—or a basket or a travel case or a treasure chest. You carry these together with the person who made the memories with you. The closer the person, the heavier the box. When that person is suddenly gone, it feels like they dropped their side of the load. It feels like you have to carry it all on your own, now that the person who knows your stories isn't here to remember them. And I don't think the memories ever get lighter. I think you get stronger. But without warning and without notice, you can get a whiff of sunscreen or cologne or spaghetti sauce; you can hear a love song on the radio or a Christmas carol at the mall or a worship song at church; and suddenly you are saying good-bye all over again.

It's a whole lot to process and deal with. That's why it takes so long. There is a time to mourn. Give it the time it needs. Be patient with you. When the light goes off in your world, don't rush to turn it back on. And when someone tries to rush you, to flip the light back on because it's easier for them, choose to forgive them—but do not obey them. They simply don't understand.

God will bring the sunshine again. Just you wait.

· · ·

With all change comes loss. Loss of time. Loss of control. Loss of power. Loss of options. Loss of consistency. Loss of relationship. Change is rarely the problem. It's the loss that comes with change that most of us don't like. My parents have said that loving me through the season of losing Robb was probably akin to loving someone who had experienced a traumatic brain injury. On the outside, I looked the same. But I processed my thoughts, my days, and my world entirely differently. It felt different to everybody. My healing was slow, and the strides were subtle.

About a year into this new normal, my mom confided in a friend of hers, "I keep waiting to see signs of who she was. I'm afraid I might never get my girl back."

In pure honesty and compassion, this wise mentor told her gently, "Truthfully, you might not. This may be who she is now." My mom recalls that moment as one of the hardest in the journey of our family. There's a long list of things that time and therapy can heal, but some changes come to stay.

My brother is like sunshine in my life. He is reliable, steady, and perpetually present. And if I look very hard into the kaleidoscope of what he means to me, it feels like I'm burning a hole into my soul. It's too hot to touch. I adore him, and his eloquent perspective on loss and change was so valuable. Rob said, "I spent years getting used to my sister's new normal. She changed so much, and we all had to learn her quiet, reserved, introverted side. I learned how to be with her, how to talk to her, the patterns of what we talk about and what we don't talk about, what makes her laugh, and what will never be funny. It sort of felt like somebody turned the family system upside down. It felt like I walked back into a room I had memorized, but now the furniture was all moved around and I didn't know where I was supposed to sit. I felt like, *Just give me a minute. I know the couch is here somewhere, and I'll find it. Nothing is where I left it. It's all new and different. Somebody shook the house like a salt shaker, and everything landed in different places. I didn't know it would look nice this way, but it really does. I'm getting used to it. I just can't find my shoes. I'm waiting to see where we'll all sit in this new living room.*"

Maybe you love someone who has been changed, altered, diagnosed, victimized, or traumatized. And maybe the wait you're in has a lot to do with being patient for them to come home, come back to you, come back to themselves. If that's where you are, your journey may feel even more hopeless and out of control. It's hard enough to control our own outcomes, but it's painfully worse to be patient for someone else's.

If you cannot understand what God is doing, either in your life or in the life of someone you love so much that you feel their pain like your own, trust that he is for us. You don't have to believe this; he won't make you. But it makes the dark nights more than a little easier if you can believe that somebody else is watching, listening, and in charge. He is on our side. He is patient. Jesus doesn't rush our sorrow. He will lead you through—not around—the valley of this shadow of death.

Please, for the sake of all the hurting hearts, be brave enough to walk in the dark.

. . .

For no one is cast off
  by the Lord forever.
Though he brings grief, he will show compassion,
  so great is his unfailing love.
For he does not willingly bring affliction
  or grief to anyone.
LAMENTATIONS 3:31-33, NIV

He will never leave you.
JOHN 14:16, TPT

*Very truly I tell you, you will weep and mourn
while the world rejoices. You will grieve, but your
grief will turn to joy. . . . Now is your time of
grief, but I will see you again and you will rejoice,
and no one will take away your joy.*
JOHN 16:20, 22, NIV

However long the night, the dawn will break.
AFRICAN PROVERB

CHAPTER 6

Walkie-Talkie Theology

When It's Not about You

For those of you with children who have grown out of car seats but are not yet allowed behind the wheel, let me let you in on the key ingredient for a little dose of freedom on a family camping trip: walkie-talkies. Trust me on this. It's a little space and independence for everybody. For our family trip to the mountains last summer, we busted out the walkie-talkies and our nicknames: Papa Bear, Queen Bee, Babe Ruth, and Hollywood. The boys headed down the hill for some evening fishing, their walkie-talkies in hand. It was 8:30 p.m., and Tucker's prayer all week long had been that he could please catch just one fish.

They had been gone for maybe ten minutes when I heard

the buzz of my walkie-talkie. "Queen Bee. Babe Ruth to Queen Bee. Roger."

I picked up my walkie-talkie and responded. "This is Queen Bee."

"You didn't say Roger."

"Roger."

"No, first you say Queen Bee, *then* Roger."

"Tucker, what do you need?"

"I just have one question. Roger."

"Yes?"

"Say, 'Yes, Roger.'"

"Tucker."

"Roger."

"Yes, Tucker. Roger."

"Good job. Here's my question. If God can put the baby Jesus inside Mary, why can't he put a little fish on my hook? Roger."

Ah, yes. An age-appropriate version of some very deep theology.

"Well, Tuck . . ."

"Babe Ruth, please. Roger."

"Well, Babe Ruth, it's hard to know. But maybe God has a different plan for that fish, and his plan doesn't involve you or your hook."

"I didn't catch that, Queen Bee."

I repeated, louder this time, "I said! *It's hard to know! Maybe God has a different plan for the* . . ."

"I cannot hear you, Queen Bee. Are you holding down

the button? Roger." I received his coaching, as if he invented walkie-talkies and I'm new at this. (*Please,* I thought. *I was chatting with Uncle Rob on these puppies before you were even a twinkle, pal.*)

"Yes, I'm holding down the button. Roger."

"Say it one more time. Roger."

"I. Think. Maybe. God. Has—"

"Queen Bee! You are breaking up! I repeat! There is a poor connection, Queen Bee! You are breaking up!"

For crying out loud. Walkie-talkies are good for many things, like freedoms and explorations of independence. Fostering discussions on the cornerstones of theology may not be one of the strengths of this technology.

"Tucker, we can talk about it when you come back up the hill."

"Roger."

"Yes. Roger."

What I wanted to tell Tucker is that maybe God has another plan for the fish. Or honestly? Maybe the fish doesn't like the squeaks and squawks of the walkie-talkies, and he swam away on his own free will.

Fish are like that. So is free will.

· · ·

Tucker's question was ultimately this one: Why won't God help me? Why won't he step in? If he has all the power of the universe, and if answering me would cost him nothing, why doesn't he help me? Anyone who's lived through any amount of waiting has likely asked this very question.

Maybe you're asking a question like this too. (Although probably about a topic much deeper than a fish on your hook.)

I've been tempted to believe that God is angry with me, that this season in my life is obviously a punishment for something. I've found myself searching my heart and my past, looking for something I could or should confess to hurry myself out of this mess.

Sometimes I've wondered if God is unfair. I begin to look around me, peering into the social-media perspectives of people who are living happy, joyful lives, and I wonder why God rewarded them with *a*, *b*, and *c* when we all know they've never given him *x*, *y*, or *z*.

In the face of my own waiting, invariably someone will say something stupid that makes me want to punch them in the neck. Like, "Praise the Lord who answers prayers! I got a great parking spot!" Or "Finally! I've been asking the Lord to put this sweater on sale, and he finally did!" Or "We weren't sure if all our IKEA furniture would fit in the minivan, but praise the Lord, it did. He answers prayers." You guys, those are not real problems. And if it seems like God is more helpful in finding lost keys or granting discounts and close parking spaces than in dealing with really difficult requests, then you may begin to feel like you want nothing to do with a God like that.

Heavy questions, seasons, and situations present a crossroads of faith, an intersection where you have a decision to make about what you will believe. Faith is won or lost, deepened or weakened. Roots grow deeper, or faith blows away like tumbleweed across a ghost town.

And the thing is, these kinds of feelings are very normal. Doubts are well within the normal range of responses when you feel like God is unaware, angry, ignoring, absent, punishing, unkind, or unfair. Who would want to obey a God who doesn't seem to know or even care? It can all start to get a little murky. Or a lot murky.

When I let my doubts go untended, the little questions can grow legs and mature into unbelief. That's the beginning of a downward spiral, because in any relationship, unbelief breaks down trust. And broken trust leads to broken intimacy. If you don't tend to the doubts, they will only grow bigger, deeper, stronger. They become a wedge between you and God, a distraction that sets you up to make decisions that will make everything worse, harder, and much more painful in the long run.

The enemy is an expert at sniffing out those times when we are weary of waiting, when we are tired and vulnerable to the seed of doubt. We can see this when Jesus went into the wilderness for forty days, and Satan met him there to tempt him.[1] Jesus, now burdened with the needs and boundaries of human flesh, was tired, hungry, and ready for God to lift the fast. Based on this encounter, we can see that Satan is persistent, clever, smart, aware of weaknesses, and cunningly opportunistic. He knows when the air changes and defenses are low.

But as we look at this encounter with Satan, we can also deduce some important things about waiting. First, a difficult season doesn't mean that you misunderstood or misheard God. Jesus came into the desert directly after he was baptized, so this long drought came directly after his finest moment with God. He had just heard God announce, "You are my dearly loved Son, and you bring me great joy."[2] He didn't mishear those words, and this season of waiting didn't negate them.

We can also see that Satan is tenacious. He comes at Jesus again and again, with opportunities and almost-truths. He doesn't give up easily, and we shouldn't expect him to back down from his mission to distract us either. That prowling lion knows what he's doing, and our impatience only gives him fresh meat to devour.

Here's one thing we can be sure of: God was with Jesus when he was in the wilderness. In fact, he abides in all of us who call on his name. He weaves this theme throughout both the Old and New Testaments. I love verses that say this very explicitly:

We find, "The LORD was with Joseph" (Genesis 39:3).

He promised Moses directly, "I will certainly be with you" (Exodus 3:12, HCSB).

To Isaac, he said, "I am the God of Abraham your father. Fear not, for I am with you" (Genesis 26:24, ESV).

He sent Joshua into battle with this promise: "Be strong and courageous. . . . I will be with you" (Deuteronomy 31:23).

When Gideon feared he was too small for the task at hand, God said, "I will be with you" (Judges 6:16).

And God repeats his important message again to his people throughout the book of Isaiah:

Fear not, for I am with you;
    be not dismayed, for I am your God;
I will strengthen you, I will help you,
    I will uphold you with my righteous right hand.[3]

I have called you by name; you are mine.[4]

We know that God doesn't play favorites, though I confess it's very hard to imagine that he loves me as much as his buddies James, David, Moses, and Job. But the fact is true whether I believe it or not, whether I feel it or not. He was with them; he is with me.

. . .

Can I get in your business here for a moment? I feel like we know each other well enough to take a step closer. Here is my question: What are you saying to yourself about this wait you are in?

I am not asking what you're saying to other people about this season. That matters, but it doesn't matter as much as the brutal honesty of your inner dialogue. That's where the power is, for better and for worse. In my season as a widow, I learned this intimately.

I found myself saying things like "I cannot do this." "I will not survive this." "My children are scarred." "We will not recover."

Depression is like this. It becomes a voice of its own, but quite cleverly, it sounds just enough like your own voice that you can begin to think it might be right.

I needed to learn to speak differently. The differences were subtle and often silent, but they mattered. I began to encourage myself with words like "I will do today." "I can give my children what they need." "My children will be men of compassion with a story to tell." "I can never make up for the loss of their dad, but I am a really great mom." "I will do the next thing, and I will do my best."

It took training. And, quite frankly, sometimes it was easier to be negative. The negative voice gave me permission to give up. But when I was really honest with myself, I realized that's not the permission I wanted. I wanted and needed permission to stay in the game, to defy the odds, to win this fight.

Your thoughts are more powerful than you think. They are more powerful than you can imagine. I think we can all agree that so much of life isn't about what happens to you—it's about how you think about it.

Would you say that your mind is controlled by the Spirit of God, consistently filled with thoughts that are honoring, constructive, and positive? Or would you say your inner dialogue is littered with thoughts that are negative, critical, and destructive? Which of these voices sounds more like you?

Consider these:

- *I am tired of waiting.*
- *This is pointless.*
- *I hate this stupid job and my stupid life.*
- *Nothing will ever change.*
- *I cannot get ahead.*
- *God has forgotten me.*
- *This will always be a problem.*
- *This will always be my problem.*

What could it look like if you sent yourself a different message?

- *Waiting is difficult, but I can do hard things.*
- *My life matters, even as I wait.*
- *I am not on hold or benched or sidelined.*
- *My mind is full of life, and my life is full of possibilities.*
- *I have divine patience to wait for what will happen next.*
- *I believe that God is in this, at work in ways I cannot see.*
- *In this season, I will make a difference with God's help.*

Here is the beauty of your inner dialogue: God can change the way you think. Thoughts have power; if repeated in our minds often enough, we begin to believe them as truth—whether they are true or not. You can let God change you by changing the way you think, by transforming your mind.[5] Choose some thoughts to tell yourself regularly, whether you believe them yet or not. (You don't have to feel courageous to tell yourself that you *are*.) You do not have to align your thoughts, but you can ask God to change your thinking.

If trust is a choice, what could it look like if you choose to trust? What if your circumstances are not an indication of God's heart for you, whether he loves you, and whether he's with you? What if the situation you find yourself in is not an indication of what God is up to? What if you choose to believe he is for you, even when it feels like he is not? What if you choose to believe he loves you, even when it feels like he doesn't?

Imagine how that could change everything.

Everything.

You may not be able to push the time line or change your circumstances, but you can change the way you think about them. And as you do so, you may become a new creation. You may have a deepening awareness—an *awakening*, if you will—that God was with you all along. And that awareness, that becoming, may have been the reason for this wait.

. . .

It's not the load that breaks you down. It's the way you carry it.
ATTRIBUTED TO LOU HOLTZ

Reflections on Longing

. . .

- What kind of "daily" waiting do you hate most? What comes easiest for you? Start a list of all that you're waiting for, the biggest of things and the smallest of things. Keep that list handy as you journey through these pages.

- Have you dealt with a difficult life circumstance that resulted from your own choices? How did you change in the waiting, for better or worse? Have a conversation on screen or paper with yourself at a much younger age. What would you advise about what lies ahead? Can you see God's presence in the "rearview mirror" of hard life events—times when he truly was there, though you may not have thought so at the time?

- Do you currently have a wait that feels like a deep ache or a longing? Put it into words—on paper or screen, or with someone you trust to listen well. Give meaning to that longing by verbalizing it, even if you're the only one who sees those words. What kind of waiting seems hardest or most frightening to you—the wait you're in, or one of the other kinds that are described in this chapter? Why? Who else in your life is in a waiting place? How can you encourage or just wait with them in ways that they can sense and feel?

- Which of the Great Waiters can you most relate to? If there is always work that can be done in the waiting, what kind of work do you think might be best designed for your journey?

- Are you in a waiting-to-start kind of place that keeps you from going after your dreams? Describe your aspirations—on screen or paper, or to someone you trust with your emotions. What can you do to make progress in this season, even if the steps are indirect?

- If you are waiting to begin, ask yourself why you are stuck in neutral. Are you putting it off because you can't figure out how you'll finish it when it gets bigger than you? Are you waiting for more instructions? Just start with the information you have. There are things you can do now, starting today, no matter what season

you are in. You can begin learning. Reading. Studying.
Imagining. Dreaming. Working on your attitude
and your relationships. Taking responsibility for your
responsibilities. Be like Noah. Concentrate on what
God has given you to do. Get started.

PART TWO
Becoming

As Peter and I sat in the rocking chairs on the deck of his family's mountain home, I asked him to tell me more about the morning after his first night in jail. He had been released to go home, but he wasn't exactly set free.

He said, "I don't know how to describe the shame. It's so thick. I wanted to avert my eyes from any human. I didn't want to look anyone in the eye, but I had to face them. I felt untouchable and pathetic, and I was so embarrassed by how I had dishonored my family. Aside from that deep shame, I had the inconvenience of losing my license for at least a year, and as for riding your bike everywhere in the middle of winter? Let's just say this: People who ride their bikes in a snowstorm are probably not environmentalists. They're likely people who got a DUI and aren't allowed to drive. I was that guy.

"But I'm an actor. I put on a facade to show everyone that this didn't bother me. Sure, I screwed up a little bit, and yes, there was alcohol involved, but that doesn't mean I'm an alcoholic. I may have some alcoholic tendencies, but calling me 'an alcoholic' is a little drastic and judgy. My sisters asked me to go to an AA meeting, and I said sure, I'd go. I wanted to appease them, and it wouldn't hurt to look good for the upcoming arraignment I had with a judge. I would take the classes and the courses so that when I went to sentencing this judge would see that I was serious about living a better life. I was highly motivated to make myself look good."

When Peter went to those first meetings, he wanted to hide in the back. As the new guy, he didn't realize that all the people in the room were in the same boat with him, on their own journeys of submission. They were there because they knew they had a problem. He was there to hide from his.

He went to as many meetings as he could, and he had a sponsor sign off on all of them, all to make him look good. He built an elaborate house of cards. He'd prove himself to be compliant, a good guy who just had a few too many drinks. He'd present his case and say, "This was hardly a pattern, your honor. Look at this exemplary behavior. Surely I am a man who is above the punishment of the law."

What Peter failed to recall was this fact: This DUI was his *third*. And the courts had recently passed a law saying that a third DUI meant mandatory jail time. It had been twenty-five years since his last DUI, but the system doesn't care how long it has been. It could be three in one week or three over the course of a lifetime. Three is three.

I've learned that there are two Greek words for time: *kairos* and *chronos*. They are subtly but importantly different. *Kairos* refers to a season or opportunity, and *chronos* refers to the actual passing of time.[1] God often presents us with opportunities to make the right decision, a chance to choose the better path. If we miss the exit signs and persist on a path of destruction, despite his gentle guidance, God is prone to shifting strategies to get our attention. This is when he uses time, days upon days and weeks upon weeks. When we ignore the season to obey, he uses the actual passage of time as a tool to change our hearts. Somehow, deep within us, there begins to grow a longing to obey.

Peter could delay the sentencing as long as possible, and he could attend as many meetings as he deemed fit to pull off this charade. He could offer additional urinalysis and he could volunteer for court-ordered classes before the court even ordered them. But it hardly mattered. He had an appointment with a judge, and there was a jail cell with Peter's name on it.

. . .

His sentencing date didn't come around on the calendar for almost a year, and the waiting was a fierce opponent. He got himself a copy of *The Big Book of Alcoholics Anonymous*, and he started the process. Actually, as he said, he fought the process. "It seemed so stupid. I didn't believe any of it. I hated the wording, and I even hated the outline of the book. I didn't think I had a problem anyway, so why bother with this nonsense? I'm a Christian, and I felt the program wasn't religious enough for me. I hid behind my church identity to say that this wouldn't work for me."

But he stuck with the program, if only to keep his charade going and to get his ducks in a row as he prepared to meet the judge. Peter and his sponsor began doing the work of the book, and every week, he began to surrender a little bit more. The program called for a lot of inventories, of putting pencil to paper and looking at his past with rigorous honesty. He didn't want to look at that guy in the mirror. He didn't want to come to terms with the fact that people without a drinking problem do not behave this way. He didn't want to use the word *alcoholic*. It was bad enough to feel the shame of no license, the shame of spending a night in jail. Must he wear this scarlet letter, too? No, thank you.

Plus, when he was honest with himself, he knew his greatest fear was a loss of his identity. Remember, Party Peter was a fun person to be around. If he couldn't drink, how could he be funny? And if he wasn't funny, what if people didn't like him anymore? If they didn't accept him, he didn't know what he would do. And this whole business of sobriety? He had stopped drinking before, but this new awareness called him to stop for more than a weekend, more than a month, more than a semester. Sobriety was a lifetime commitment he wasn't sure he could make. He wasn't sure he wanted to.

His day in court arrived, and he carried proof of all his good decisions into the courtroom. He just wanted it to be over, and he was ready for the judge to see his exemplary work and ask him only to pay a fine.

Peter said, "But then she told me, 'You've got sixty days in jail and six months on home arrest.' To say it was 'a punch in the gut' was too cliché for what I felt. I had to try not to break down right there in the courtroom. I had to report to jail. We had a date. And my sentencing would include Christmas Day. It was surreal. I got everything I did not wish for. For the first time in my life, there was no way around it."

One of his sisters drove him to jail. He watched her expression as they cuffed him—her only brother. The shame overwhelmed him yet again. He hadn't done this just to himself but also to the people who loved him most in the world. That was more than he could bear, even more painful than the tight cuffs on his wrists.

As a coping mechanism, Peter claimed a new mental approach: Get this over with as soon as possible. He received his jumpsuit, his jail sandals, a fitted sheet for the plastic mattress, two blankets, a towel, something resembling a toothbrush, and a spork he would need to bring to any meal. He had seen plenty of movies that painted some horrific visions of what happens in jail, so he decided to try keeping to himself. He was sent to the second floor, a pod filled with sixty men.

He said, "They put me in a cell with a guy who was older than me, and I don't know how long he'd been there. I had to take the top bunk, and I'd say it was maybe twenty-four inches wide, made of steel. I got two blankets, no pillow. The nights were filled with the sounds of snoring and sleeping men, but there were also sounds I'd never heard before, like the clinking of doors. I heard stories right away of a guy who had fallen off his top bunk and snapped his ankle, so even in resting there were risks. I tried to just get whatever sleep I could, keep quiet, and learn my way around. They had a little book cart, so I found an AA book to read, and I learned I could request a Bible through the messaging system. There was so much alone time. So much down time. So much wasted time."

He quickly learned that one of the indignities of jail is the loss of the conveniences that come with freedom. A pillow. A comb. Sunshine, a breeze. Chap Stick. His lips were so cracked and chapped. We don't realize it's a privilege to moisturize our skin; the chapped lips were an unexpected emotional toll that pushed him to a ragged edge.

As soon as he had the opportunity, Peter applied for work release—and, to his great relief, permission was granted. There was a great deal of envy in his pod because work release brought a small margin of freedom to leave during the day. He could leave at 7:00 in the morning, and he had to return by 8:30 at night. He got a new costume—a green jumpsuit—and he got his own cell, with a bed made of cement instead of steel. He got a bracelet on his ankle, so they could track his location at all times, and if he wasn't back in time for curfew, he could expect to hear sirens screaming out to find him. He got twelve hours of pseudofreedom for five days a week, a chance to get a real cup of coffee, and access to a simple tube of Chap Stick. A breath of liberty, indeed.

He found a rhythm for his weekdays in jail.

Get up at sunrise.

Check out the very moment you're allowed.

Walk out of jail and hope someone is there to pick you up at 7:00 in the morning. (His sisters set up a spreadsheet with times, dates, and volunteers who loved Peter and were willing to help him get these few hours of freedom and work. I love this part of Peter's story, about the friends and family who surprised him by signing up, those who took him through the Starbucks drive-through, and those who brought him a most coveted snack to eat in the car: an apple or a pear.) As a professional recruiter, he'd clock in to work from his apartment, spending the day conducting interviews via phone calls and virtual appointments that didn't require him to be physically present. At the end of the work day, he'd clock out and head back to jail for the check-in process. Just in case he had grown accustomed to his small window of freedom, there was an officer waiting to conduct a strip search before he could enter lockdown again at the end of the day. There was no question who was in charge, and it wasn't Peter.

CHAPTER 7

Honesty in the Waiting
When Truth Is All You Have

Robb had been gone for maybe two weeks when the boys and I packed up for a trip back to Ohio. I moved to Colorado in my early twenties, and my soul took root right away. My soul breathes deep in Colorado air, but my heart still feels at home in Ohio, with the smell of cut grass in the summer, the changing leaves in the autumn, the snow that stays so long it turns gray in the winter, and the grand openings of ice-cream stands in the spring. My sons, my parents, and I made a pilgrimage back to the Midwest because that is home for us. An important part of me exhales in the safe presence of my many cousins and the magical healing power of my aunt Joyce's banana cake. When everything fell apart because the other half of my marriage had died, we packed up and we went to Ohio. Because of course. You fix what you can fix.

I remember putting the boys to sleep one night on the pull-out couch in my aunt Janet's basement. I would later join them, or rather, I would later *move them* to their sleeping bags on the floor when I was ready for bed myself. Something seemed to ease the bedtime routine when they got to start out in my bed. They knew they'd better be quiet and obedient, since they felt they were getting away with something.

I should tell you that I have never in my life quite gotten over the precious everything of my boys when they are sleeping. No matter what has gone wrong during the day, no matter how great the tantrums and transgressions, there is no wrong that could not be made right by the sight of a little boy sound asleep in his footie pajamas. The gentle snoring. The fluttering of dreaming eyelashes. The satin blanket balled into his dimpled, baby-boy fist. The smell of Johnson's baby shampoo from his bedtime bath. Or almost as endearing, the salty scent of sleeping baby sweat. The rosy pink cheeks did me in every time.

I came to move them from the couch to the floor, and as I always did, I stopped to breathe them in. I leaned close to Tyler, bringing my nose close to breathe his baby air and to feel his feathery breath on my cheek. And suddenly, the scent of his clean hair, coupled with his little blue footie pajamas—the ones he now wore day in and day out—it all multiplied and compounded and washed over me in a wave of grief that took my breath away. My breath poured out of me in a long, silent, heaving sob. It emptied me so completely that I knew my recovering intake of breath would be enough to wake the boys. I was out of control, swept over the edge of the facade of holding it together. I grabbed at the blanket, and I stuffed it into my mouth just as the sob climbed on top of me. It was roaring. I rode this wave of grief, rocking myself as I wept silently into the blanket I held with one hand, my other hand hovering over the steady rise and fall of Tyler's back as he slept. I wanted to soothe him, or maybe I wanted to protect him from the reality he could not yet understand.

I remember thinking, *My God, what have you done to us? What have you done to my family? To my sons? My babies? You took away their father! What were you thinking? What have you done, dear God?*

I didn't move them from the pull-out couch because what was the point, really? I let them stay. I went back upstairs to a corner of the couch in the sunken living room. I opened my journal for the first time since Robb died.

I wrote, *Okay. I am here. Let's talk. I want to believe you are good. I want to trust you. But everything is wrong. And you could have kept all of this from happening. I want to believe you are in this. I want to trust you. So we have to be honest with each other. And honestly, I don't know where you are. And I don't know why you thought this was a good idea.*

I started with honesty. I wrote it all down. And I sat in the tension of pouring it all out to a void of silence, knowing no answers would come right away, maybe not for a very, very long time. But I knew that my honesty was not nothing. Honesty was all I felt I had, the only offering I could give.

Poured out, I closed my journal, and I went back

downstairs to that pull-out couch. I crawled in between the little boy in the footie pajamas and his brother dressed like Buzz Lightyear. I fell asleep to the silence of their innocent breaths, the deep rest of children who trust.

. . .

For the first year after Robb was gone, Starbucks was my sanctuary. Every morning, I took my children to preschool, and then I took my Bible and my journal to the corner table at Starbucks. I needed a place to go that wasn't my house. If I stayed home, everything would overwhelm me, and I would go back to bed. If I had any hope of staying out of bed, then I needed to stay out of the house.

The scent of coffee beans comforts me. After being there so many hours for so many days, I became so saturated with that scent; even my laptop—a nonporous object—smelled like coffee beans. Starbucks was so wonderfully familiar. The smell, the menu, the green aprons. A place that isn't your home, but that feels as wonderfully familiar as home, is good and healing for the soul. That was my season of a "decaf grande salted caramel latte," wonderfully perfect every time.

So I took my Bible and a journal and a collection of pens. I didn't know what to say or how to say it, but I needed to do something with my hands and my thoughts, so I began copying the Psalms into my journal. I started with Psalm 1, and I worked my way through the songs and poems of the psalmists, writing down any collection of words that spoke to me. While I waited to find my praise, I borrowed from the psalmists. While I waited to find my voice, I borrowed from the psalmists. While I waited to even know what questions to ask, I borrowed from the psalmists.

I discovered quickly that every emotion is on display in the book of Psalms. I could find anger, joy, sadness, praise, lament, and questions. So many questions. More than twenty times, the psalmists asked the question *why*, including bold questions directed straight to God. Like, "Why have you forgotten me?" (Psalm 42:9) and the very bold, "Wake up, Lord! Why are you sleeping?" (Psalm 44:23, csb). God, in his great mercy, created us with a release valve for our pain: our mouths. And when we face our pain by crying out to him with our questions, he is gracious to let us speak.

I also found the beautiful companionship of the word *when*. Because in those years of the long, gray winter of my soul, the greatest strain on my faith has not always been in believing that God is in this. Sometimes the heartache has been in the waiting. That's why I feel like the psalmist understands this kind of life as he cries out over and over, "When??"

"How long, Lord? Will you forget me forever?"[1]
"Lord, how long will You look on?"[2]
"How long will the wicked celebrate?"[3]

I deeply love the desperation in David's voice when he penned Psalm 13:

O Lord, how long will you forget me? Forever?
How long will you look the other way?
How long must I struggle with anguish in my soul,
    with sorrow in my heart every day?
How long will my enemy have the upper hand?

PSALM 13:1-2

(Sometimes when I read about enemies, I have to keep in mind that David lived a life of battle. He had real enemies that prowled like lions in search of an opportunity to take his life. Thankfully, I don't live in that kind of tension or physical threat. But enemies are not only those we can see. Depression can be my enemy. Pride. Impatience. Ego. When I encounter the word *enemy*, sometimes I plug in one of those words instead. I most assuredly need God's help to keep depression, pride, impatience, and ego from getting the upper hand.)

David asked the hard questions. It means I can too. The thing is, a wait isn't terribly difficult at the beginning. It can even feel heroic while the food supplies are still strong, the tent is dry, and the blankets are clean, so to speak. But as a journey stretches long, it can be physically and emotionally taxing. There comes a point when you're so far into the middle that you can't see where you started and you can't yet see your way home. The middle place is fertile ground for hard questions. That time is the hardest.

But in just a few verses, David's tone seems to change. In a dramatic shift, he suddenly writes,

But I trust in your unfailing love.
    I will rejoice because you have rescued me.
I will sing to the LORD
    because he is good to me.

PSALM 13:5-6

There was a time when I struggled with this dramatic shift, when I felt like I couldn't relate to the mood swings from one verse to another. But now that I have walked the winding path of this kind of emotional spectrum, I think David needed to start by clearing the air, by saying what needed to be said.

My current favorite TV show is *This Is Us*, because I've always been a sucker for a good dramedy with a complex plot and a cast of endearing characters in a large family. The writing is brilliant, and the way they unfold the time line is mind-blowing. I love that show for a dozen reasons, and sometime, we should really discuss it over a cup of coffee or Facebook fan page. (The only time I don't love it is when they're exploring the sudden death of Jack, Rebecca's husband. That seems like a good time to set some emotional boundaries, since I've already lived that reality, thanks.)

But I do love the Pearsons, especially Randall and Beth. There is an episode where they're navigating some difficult parenting with their foster daughter, and just before they go into her bedroom for the big confrontation, Randall suggests that they play the "Worst-Case Scenario" game. The game is simple: Each person takes a turn to say all the things they're thinking, with no judgment, no censorship. They volley back and forth, saying the worst things that could happen, so they can set those fears aside and tackle the truth of their reality. It's the game I didn't realize I needed in my life.

Sometimes you just have to name the disappointment out loud. There are times in any relationship when we need to clear the air, when we need to say the very things we are trying so hard not to say. David does that very thing in Psalm 13, when he speaks his greatest fears. *Have you forgotten me? Am I even on your radar? Will this last forever, this anguish in my soul?*

The frustrations are all there inside us. The questions, impatience, disappointments, and accusations are all there. Pretending we don't feel that way only hurts us more—and it doesn't surprise God. We aren't protecting him from how we feel, because he already knows. I decided long ago that if I can believe that he created me, and if my emotions and questions are part of who I am, then I must also believe they are no surprise to him. One who is big enough to create me must also be powerful enough to handle my questions. He is stronger than the storm.

My friend Jason Hague wrote an astoundingly honest and powerful memoir called *Aching Joy*, where he detailed his intimate faith journey through the Land of Unanswered Prayer after his son was diagnosed with severe autism. Jason is a modern-day psalmist, and he knows the brutal tension of honesty with God. He wrote, "We think God will hear our hearts' cries if only we sanitize them. But in the act of sanitization, we prove we do not trust him, as if he could only handle the sugar-coated prayers."[4]

I believe the Lord gave David a new song because he started with honesty. When you don't feel like you can be honest, then all you can think about is the thing you cannot, must not say. So clear the pipeline. Say what you're not saying. Make way for a fresh perspective. He's a big enough God to hold all the pieces, and he already knows how you feel. Might as well say it out loud.

When you present yourself with honesty, I wonder if the Lord delights. If he opens his hands to hold all the pieces, and if maybe he says, "Yes. That's what I was waiting for. I can work with this. Let's get started."

. . .

Let all that I am wait quietly before God,
for my hope is in him.
He alone is my rock and my salvation,
my fortress where I will not be shaken.
My victory and honor come from God alone.
He is my refuge, a rock where no enemy can
reach me.
O my people, trust in him at all times.
Pour out your heart to him,
for God is our refuge.
PSALM 62:5-8

We don't have to have God's answers to have His comfort.

LYSA TERKEURST[5]

If we want to wait well and experience all God has for us in the midst of our waiting, we have to be honest with Him about our fears and struggles. We also have to ask Jesus to give us eyes to see through a lens of hope and a heart molded by faith that He is working for our good and His glory.

RENEE SWOPE, IN THE FOREWORD OF *WAIT AND SEE* BY WENDY POPE

Honesty with God is the beginning of healing. . . . We must come out of our hiding places.

JASON HAGUE, *ACHING JOY*

CHAPTER 8

The Frat House, Meditation, and Testicles

The Best Strategy for Waiting

We gave the boys new Bibles for Easter, because it was time. They needed to graduate to a version that doesn't say "Little Boy's Bible" on the cover or entice them with animated drawings of someone who may or may not look like Jesus or Moses or Daniel or Joshua. The new editions are leather bound, different from each other, and will grow with them in the next few years, until they are ready for an even more sophisticated version.

I released myself from the ever-present question I ask when I buy books for my sons: "Will they really read it?" It's a fair question in the intoxicating aisles of Barnes and Noble, but it's fair to say that "whether or not they'll read it" should never be the deciding factor for whether you give or don't give a person a Bible. So they have new Bibles. And, God love them, they sniffed the inside of the spines when they opened their new Bibles. (These are my children.)

(It's possible they've watched me all their years and they think that's protocol for new books, come to think of it.)

So we have a new routine of reading our Bibles together just before bedtime. It's 8:30 p.m., and if we were really going to do this well, we would have started a half hour ago. But it is what it is. Get your Bibles, gentlemen.

I have high hopes for giving them a stronger Bible knowledge, of equipping them with some Old and New Testament literacy, of having some old-school sword drills, of giving them shiny silver dollars for verses memorized. As always, my hopes and expectations soar. But then we all sit down together, too late in the evening, and it doesn't go the way I have in mind. It's all very . . . well, age appropriate.

"Guys, since Grandma is recovering from her shoulder surgery, let's look up some verses about healing. Look in the back of your Bible, where it looks like a dictionary. That's called a concordance, and it's where you can find a list of verses with specific words."

"How do you spell *heal* again?"

"H-e-a-l."

"Oh. I thought it was h-e-l-l."

"Nope."

"I like to look at the maps, Mom."

"They're pretty cool. See if you can find the word *heal*."

"I found the word *hell.*"

"We're looking for any version of *heal, healed,* or *healing.*"

"Here's one, Mom. Leviticus 13:18-19."

But I've forgotten about the learning curve of the process:

1. finding the word in the concordance,
2. reading the reference,
3. finding the table of contents,
4. finding the page number,
5. locating the actual page,
6. finding the chapter,
7. forgetting which verse,
8. going back to the concordance,
9. losing your page, and
10. starting back at number 1.

God bless it all and give me grace.

Just when I've lost hope, he finds it and reads aloud, "'If anyone has a boil on the skin that has started to heal, but a white swelling or a reddish white spot develops in its place, that person must go to the priest to be examined.' Ew, Mom. That one's gross."

"That one is gross. Let's see what else we can find."

Return to steps 1-10, on repeat.

"Here's one, Mom. Micah 1:9. 'For my people's wound is too deep to heal.' Do you think Grandma's wound is too deep to heal? Why can't Jesus heal it?"

"He can and he will. It's not that kind of wound. Let's see
. . . how about . . ." I am more than ready to hijack this parade.

"Here's one, Mom. Hosea 7:1. 'I want to heal Israel, but
its sins are too great.' Yikes, Mom."

"Right. Let's maybe switch gears. I'll find a verse for you."

And now, with all the questions and page turning, it's
8:50, which is twenty minutes past bedtime, and I'm asking myself how hard it is to find a verse we can claim about
healing and reminding myself that Lesson Planning 101
calls for a few minutes of preparation. Perhaps I could have
looked up the verse in advance and pointed them to it, but
then this is also what some education philosophers call *open-
ended lesson plans*, and they're learning things I didn't script.
(Apparently, I call forth a lot from my education-theory
classes in moments like this one. Because I definitely didn't
script this.)

I take the reins. "Guys, look up Psalm 103."

"It starts with *S*?"

"No, it starts with *P*."

"*P* is for Psalms? That's weird."

"Yes. I know. I can't fix everything. Go back to the first
pages where it has a list of the books of the Bible. It's a table
of contents that will tell you where to find it."

"Mom, why are your books in a different order from mine?"

"Because mine is a chronological Bible."

"His starts with 2 Chronicles."

"No, it doesn't. They all start with Genesis."

"But Second Monocles is at the top of his page."

"That's because you're looking at the top of the second column in the table of contents. And it's not Monocles. It's Chronicles. Guys, let's skip this search and go instead to Philippians, chapter two."

"Is Philippians the same as Philemon?"

"Why does mine have four Johns?"

"Shouldn't Song of Songs be Song of Solomon?"

"I want to look at the maps again."

"You guys! Enough with the maps, already!" And then I'm annoyed with myself for losing my cool during family devotions, of all times. Deep breath. "Sorry, guys. I love the dialogue. I do. But please, just find Philippians."

And before we know it, it's 9:15, and we still haven't prayed for my mom's healing or even collectively found Philippians.

I finally take their Bibles, flip to Philippians 2, and ask them to read verses three and four aloud. Something about not being selfish. Let's tack that to the bathroom mirror and refrigerator door, shall we?

And of course, there is Peter, love of my life and laughter of my soul, who is incurably-forever-and-always the classic class clown, even when his wife is the proverbial teacher and the classroom is our living room. "Gentlemen, I shall now read in the original Aramaic." Insert his made-up language for Philippians 2.

(He makes me laugh every single day. His joy keeps me light, and he reminds me we are all learning, all of this, all of us, together.)

God, step into our silly, messy mess. We really have no idea what we're doing.

. . .

One year, in an ambitious fit of New Year's resolutions, and clearly on a day when we had forgotten how miserable it can be to read the Bible as a family, Peter and I decided to tackle a family challenge: Together, the four of us would memorize a verse from every book of the Bible. We decided we would take turns, working our way through the Bible and the weeks of the calendar. There are sixty-six books and fifty-two weeks, so sometimes we would double up. Whoever had that week got to choose the verse. Since we believe that there are no bad verses in the Bible, that all of them are put there for a reason, the person whose turn it was would get to lead our family in the verse they'd chosen.

The book of Leviticus happened to fall on the week when it was Tucker's turn. And so, with all of that said, and with a healthy dose of awkward, I present to you the verse we all had to memorize together.

You must not offer to the LORD an animal whose testicles are bruised, crushed, torn or cut.
LEVITICUS 22:24, NIV

Yep. Okay, so. Testicles.
I said to them, "Guys, if we're going to memorize this one,

then tell me this. What is the lesson in this verse? What can we be thankful for?"

I have to be honest, I was fishing for answers. I was looking for words like *grace*. I was looking for somebody to say how great it is that Jesus gave himself for us so we don't have to sacrifice animals and obey hundreds of laws on a daily basis.

"We can be thankful . . . that our balls aren't bruised or crushed or torn or cut."

"True. . . . Anything else?"

"Well, Mom, back then, animals were like money. And God wants the best of what we have, not our leftovers. So God didn't want people to give him things that were useless. Or, you know. Bruised."

Sure, yes. I'll take that. Firstfruits and whatnot.

There was a lot of talk about testicles at our house that week. Including bedtime prayers. "God, I promise not to give you bad testicles." Amen and amen.

(I do think Leviticus 22:24 is solidly in place in their memory.)

(And I live in a frat house.)

. . .

That was a whole lot of silliness, and all of it was true. Hold on to all of that, and let's turn the corner just a bit to some more truth with no silliness at all. As I'm writing this book about waiting, I think I have found the heart of waiting well: It is in claiming and memorizing and recalling Scripture.

We can memorize it on our own or together, as we tried at our dinner table (either successfully or not, depending on the viewpoint). We can meditate on it to let it soak into our minds. We can recall it by reading it while we wait in the dentist's office or repeating it out loud while we wait at the stoplight. We can lean on it in difficult seasons of loss, grief, brokenness, and healing. We can trust in its faithfulness as a lifeline through times of favor, praise, wonder, and—of course—waiting.

The Word of God is living and active, sharper than any double-edged sword. It is pure and perfect, inspired by God. It will light your path and set you free.[1] The words of Scripture provide encouragement, comfort, and strength. The truths can break our old habits and set us free to new patterns. Scripture gives us hope, joy, and patience. And when you get to know the writers and the one they've written about, you can grow to love them and their stories, and to begin to feel like you know them. I promise you this: Recalling Scripture is the very best way to wait for time to pass, whether it's just a few minutes or a long season.

Sometimes the hearing alone can resonate. But the blessing is in the *doing*. It's when the inscription meets my actions, when my thoughts match the words. This is when there is blessing and power in the words: when I do them. When I remember them, when I lean on the power in them, when I repeat them to myself in the darkest hour of the night, when I speak these words over my children, though they know not yet what they mean, the words fill the space around them and the Word of God does not return void.

. . .

Once upon a time, I accidentally attended a Buddhist retreat. It was actually a writer's retreat, but the instructor was a practicing Buddhist, so the retreat carried some strong Eastern influence. I'm not Buddhist, and some might say it was unwise and even dangerous to subject myself to the practices of a faith so different from my own. Certainly, I was aware of the differences. But I was also—I *am* also—aware that greater is he who is in me than he who is in the world[2] or even in that room. I would take him with me. We go everywhere together.

Each morning of our retreat, we began with meditation— thirty minutes of silence when the instructor guided us to clear our minds and become completely present. I wanted to be good at it, mostly because there is a solid part of me that will always want to do as I am instructed and show my teacher that I am teachable. Part of me always wants to be the star pupil. So I tried.

But I wasn't good at it, not the way they did it. I could focus on my breath, yes. In and out. In and out. But I could not seem to make myself one with the rocks outside my window. I could not hear the curiosity of the trees. I could not anchor my awareness in the soles of my feet. They were feet. On the floor. I was failing at meditation.

And then I remembered where else I had heard that word *meditate*. Ah, yes—in Scripture! The psalmists were meditators!

O God, we meditate on your unfailing love.[3]

I will meditate on your majestic, glorious splendor
　　and your wonderful miracles.[4]

Help me understand the meaning of your
　　commandments,
　　　and I will meditate on your wonderful deeds.[5]

Study this Book of Instruction continually. Meditate
on it day and night so you will be sure to obey
everything written in it.[6]

So maybe I wasn't supposed to try to become one with the grass. Maybe I couldn't trust my own presence. I know my heart is deceptive and distracted, and trusting my own way is dangerous. Perhaps I could spend this time directing my thoughts to the presence of truth instead of to the presence of myself.

I took the one thing of theirs that made sense to me: the breathing in and out. Instead of anchoring my awareness in the arches of my feet, I anchored my thoughts in the Word of the Lord, the Maker of heaven and earth.

I chose the portion of the first verse that came to my mind: "*Be strong and courageous! . . . For the* LORD *your God is with you wherever you go.*"[7]

It's one of our family verses, on display in the dining room. I made up a little ditty to teach it to the boys when they were three and five years old, when it was time to step back into our lives from our trip to Ohio after Robb had died. I felt so afraid of everything. I needed this truth as much as they did. We all know it now.

I gave each word my full attention. I breathed in and out. And I explored the depth of every word on the rise and fall of my breaths.

Be. Just be. Be here. Be you. Be in this moment. Don't go anywhere else in your mind. Just be. Be here now.

Strong. Solid oak tree, planted by the river. Strong back. Strong legs. Strong muscles. Strong lioness.

And. This word means there is more. There is something else I am instructed to be. Wait for it. It comes on the next breath.

Courageous. Brave. Unflinching. Forward. Immovable.

For. It means *because.* There is a reason I am called— commanded!—to be strong and courageous. There is a reason that I can be those things.

The. The one and only. T-H-E. The Maker of heaven and earth. The God Who Sees. The One. The Great I Am.

Lord. King of kings. Lord of lords. He who sits on the throne. The earth is his footstool.

Your. Mine. My God. He belongs to *me.* I belong to him. He is mine. I am his.

God. Capital G. The Beginning and the End.

Is. Present tense. Here now. Here. Now. The Great I Am is in this moment.

With. I am not alone.

You. Me. He knows my name.

Wherever. Here. There. Everywhere. He hems me in, behind and before. He goes before me. I cannot go anywhere outside his presence. He is Wherever.

You. Me. Tricia.

Go. Action word. Go. Take the next step. I can do this. He is with me.

I repeated my breaths and these words. I meditated. When the instructor rang the bell twice, the signal to finish, I opened my eyes, refreshed and renewed. The other writers may have been one with the trees. But I had spent time with the Lord.

. . .

I carry a brown leather bag with me at all times. It is filled with the collection of nonnegotiable items that I must carry with me—like I said, at all times. If you peek inside my bag, you'll find two or three books, a notebook, a handful of colorful pens, and a Ziploc bag of 3 × 5 cards. There is a reason I carry all of these so habitually (sometimes obsessively): It's because I hate waiting.

Few things feel more futile to me than a break in my day with nothing to do. So I carry this emergency kit with me, just in case the day opens up in an unexpected way. When I have my brown bag with me, waiting becomes a joy. I call it Found Time: the few minutes I have found in the corners of my day.

When my children were small, I felt like every moment

of my life was accounted for, and it all belonged to someone else. (Two someones.) I couldn't find much time for myself, and that made me feel like I wasn't spending much time with God. I know now that mothering small people is a spiritual practice of selflessness all its own, but I didn't get that when I was in the throes of it. I just felt busy with things that never stayed finished, and I felt guilty for never getting the right things done.

Toni Morrison, a prolific and award-winning novelist, once wrote of her experiences as writer and single mom of two young boys. She said she found time to write "in the edges of the day." There is gold to be found in those stolen moments, and the key is to be ready. Have a plan for your Found Time. Waiting doesn't have to feel like sand slipping through an hourglass. It can feel instead like treasures falling into your open hands.

One day, I wrote one verse on a 3 × 5 card. (3 × 5 cards are a few of my favorite things. "Raindrops on roses / And whiskers on kittens . . ." and colorful pens and 3 × 5 cards.) I put the card in my back pocket for the day, and I pulled it out when any unexpected moment of freedom crept into the day. I read the words aloud to my children when we waited at stoplights, the two of them riding along in their car seats, holding sippy cups and pacifiers. They were probably too small to understand, but I wanted to believe in the tender soil of their hearts, ready to receive these truths. I read the card silently to myself in the waiting room at the pediatrician's office. In line at the grocery store. On a park bench during a playdate. Any time I had a few moments to wait, I was ready with my waiting plan.

A collection of these cards began growing, and I gathered them in a sandwich baggie.

On the morning when Robb got so suddenly sick, I waited in the kitchen while my bedroom was crowded with paramedics working to restore his heart, his lungs, his life. It was the longest wait of my life. But I had my waiting plan. I got out my Ziploc sandwich bag, and I read through my verses again. When the paramedics delivered the news that he had died, the card in my hand read,

> I lift up my eyes to the mountains—
>   where does my help come from?
> My help comes from the LORD,
>   the Maker of heaven and earth.[8]

In the coming weeks, I held tightly to those words. They began coming to mind in the active moments of my life, not just the still ones. The words came to me when the cards weren't in front of me. My waiting plan had allowed these words to take root—and not like fragile flowers. More like oak trees.

Memorization allows us to meditate because Scripture soaks into our bones. When we are stuck in the waiting, when truth seems hard to find, we can draw on what we've written into our minds in preparation for this very season. It's a bold statement, but I dare say it's true: Scripture is the best strategy for any wait in front of you, whether you're facing a few minutes, a few months, or a whole lifetime.

(And you just might learn a thing or two about testicles.)

. . .

I know of no other single practice in the Christian life more rewarding, practically speaking, than memorizing Scripture. . . . No other single exercise pays greater spiritual dividends! Your prayer life *will be strengthened.* Your witnessing *will be sharper and much more effective.* Your counseling *will be in demand.* Your attitudes and outlook *will begin to change.* Your mind *will become alert and observant.* Your confidence and assurance *will be enhanced.* Your faith *will be solidified.*

CHARLES R. SWINDOLL,
GROWING STRONG IN THE SEASONS OF LIFE

CHAPTER 9

Passing Time with a Pen
The Beauty of Writing It Down

Left to my own devices, I'd buy more pens every time I buy milk. I collect them obsessively. Never too many pens. That's my rule.

I pass time with a pen. It's true on a number of levels. In small moments, I doodle in the margins of books and on airplane napkins. In more intentional moments, I write in my planner to document the day. I write in my journal to capture ideas. If I'm out and about without a pen, I can feel like someone has cut off my hands. Without fail, I'll need to write something down, and I'll have no tools for the task. (Or, someone with good intentions will hand me a ballpoint specimen of worthlessness, like the free ones from the bank. As if that counts as a writing instrument I can use.) It's kind of a phobia, the fear of penlessness. The struggle is real.

But in all seriousness, I've found a pen to be a good tool for wading through the wait. Now, please don't get scared. Before you think this is a chapter about journaling, written by a writer who doesn't understand that other people think and process differently, stay with me. I want to tell you a few of my favorite strategies, and they don't all involve logging long hours of scrawling your thoughts.

In Habakkuk 2:2, the Lord said, "Write down the revelation" (NIV). He said this because he knows our natural tendency to forget. At best, we have a strong propensity to misremember. A pen is a great tool against the facts that fade with time, and I've learned that it is a great guide to mark the very passing of it as well.

A few years ago, I discovered the discipline of circle prayers. Mark Batterson introduced the world to this practice,[1] and his storytelling made it come to life. He wrote about Honi, a sage who lived outside the walls of Jerusalem in the first century BC. A devastating drought had crippled the land, and it threatened to destroy an entire generation of people. They needed water. Honi was known for praying for rain, and he was their only hope.

Honi brought his six-foot staff into town with him, and he drew a meticulous circle in the sand. Kneeling boldly in the center of the circle, Honi called down the rain. He prayed aloud to the Lord of the universe, and he promised not to move outside that circle until the rain came down on these people and their land.

Mark wrote, "Then it happened. As his prayer ascended to the heavens, raindrops descended to the earth."[2] But Honi was not satisfied by a few raindrops. He boldly asked for more. As the sprinkling turned into a torrential downpour, Honi stayed and prayed inside his circle. The rain soaked the land, and their spirits were soaked in faith. The circle he drew in the sand became a symbol of power. Sometimes you have to stand in the circle and make your requests known to the God Who Sees, the Lord Who Listens.

I read Mark's book in a time when my church family had encountered a crisis, and there was nothing I could do to fix it. I could only pray. How odd it is that we tend to offer that when we have nothing left to give, when really that's the heartbeat of all there is. I can always pray.

So I began praying differently. I wrote down just a few words at a time, and I circled them with my trusty pen every day. There is nothing magical about drawing the circle, but it gave me something to do with my hands, something to watch on the page, as I prayed for big things. I didn't expect this bonus, but the discipline also gave me a way to measure the passing of time. I watched the circles pile on top of one another. The circle grew darker and thicker until the individual lines became one bold, dark band of fortitude. I had before me a visual representation of long obedience.

This discipline changed my life. Now, several years later, I'm still circling—many things every day. There were some seasons when it felt like my prayers weren't going any higher than the ceiling, but I needed to keep circling. There are things I circle with the knowledge that I will never stop circling them, not as long as my hand can hold a pen. I ask God to protect my children and the schools they each attend. I ask him to give me an awakening to understand Scripture. I ask for wisdom. I'm asking God to send these things, and I watch to see how he answers.

Some things I am circling will have a clear and definite finish line. I have asked for a spouse for my single friend who longs to share her life with a companion. I have prayed for work for my parents in seasons of unemployment; I have asked that God would give them the perfect jobs to match their skills and that he would bless the work of their hands. I've asked God to forgive my financial mistakes and equip us with additional income that will get us out of debt. I have prayed for a friend to find sobriety. I've prayed for another friend's husband to come back home to her. Each of these prayers has a specific finish line. I will know when we have crossed it.

Especially with things like these, I have begun adding tally marks. It's a way of collecting the days and showing the march of time. I can remind myself how long I have stayed in the waiting game. Forty-one days. Seventy-eight days. Six hundred and fourteen days.

It may seem like it would be discouraging to see the days pile up, but I've found just the opposite to be true. The tally marks show a measure of focus and loyalty. When I start to think, *God isn't doing anything with this one. I should stop asking,* I can counter my own skepticism by counting the tally marks. It's akin to looking back on a map that shows how far we've come. "Eighty-three days? We can't stop now. Not when we've come this far."

I keep all these circles in one bound journal with colorful tabs to show which ones still need my attention, which journeys I'm currently walking. I pray them every day. And best of all, when I see a prayer answered, I know just what to do: I open to that journal page, and I write today's date. I mark the finish line. I can stop asking for this one, because God said yes. I asked, I waited, he answered. I close my eyes and take a breath filled with gratitude. I notice that he heard me.

Sometimes he gives me a clear no. There are times when his word is final, when I feel like I can imagine him saying (just like I say to my kids about some of their requests), "You can keep asking, but it's a hard no on this one. I'm not changing my mind."

When I get a solid answer—sometimes yes, sometimes no—I take the tab off that page. It doesn't need my patience or attention anymore, but it serves as a reminder of the journey. The asking. The waiting. The answer. The gratitude. The finish lines.

And then I move the tab to the next empty page, an invitation to stay in the game. To watch for the next big ask. To wait for the next big answer.

Another way I pass the time with a pen is by writing

letters. Sometimes I write them to a person I'm waiting to meet, sometimes I write them to myself, and other times I write more abstractly, writing letters to an idea or a season or a farewell. During long periods of waiting, this practice of capturing the thoughts in my head and the desires of my heart on the page has effectively guided my energy into a fruitful sense of active waiting, rather than a frustrated passivity.

(Right now, you may be thinking, *But I've never liked writing letters. I'm not good with words, my hand gets tired, and I don't even like my handwriting.* Fair enough. But please, let me remind you that a paragraph from the heart is still a letter. Words that nobody reads can still be a letter. And even if you're the only one who ever reads your words, letter writing may still become a useful tool for clarifying your thoughts.)

I wrote letters to each of my babies when I was pregnant with them.

Dear Baby,

You are just a few days old in there. You have a heartbeat and spinal cord, and your cells are multiplying like crazy. You are becoming. I am over the moon excited about you, little one. I sure am tired.

Love, Mommy

Dear Child of Mine,

You are a boy! I cannot wait to meet you. Fire trucks, overalls, and baseball caps. I started collecting them all for you. A Boy.

When I called your Uncle Rob to tell him I was having another boy, his first words were, "You will be so protected."

I'm a mom of boys. Who knew I could love blue so much?

Love, Mom

I wrote letters during each pregnancy, and to my great heartbreak, two of those babies died before they were born. I have two journals with letters to my babies who I never got to hold. We all know that not everything we ask for comes to be. Not everything we wait for becomes ours to keep, and some dreams evaporate before they take root. But the wait mattered to me. Those pages hold the story of my broken heart. I loved those babies, I wanted each of those children, and my heart had reason to be sad.

When Robb died, I read those journals again. I had always wanted four children, and it occurred to me then that we shared them in our separate places: two with me, two with him. The penned pages remind me that it happened. All of it.

. . .

In the years while I waited for Peter and me to find one another, I wrote letters to him. The first page of that notebook says, "Letters to you, though I do not know your name." I wrote letters to him for months, sometimes just a sentence or two.

Dear You,

> *It's raining today. I love gray days the most.*
> *There's freedom to do nothing.*
> *I want to do nothing with you.*
> *Let's do that soon.*

Tricia

I made nachos tonight. That could be our late-night snack.
> *I hope you like nachos. I make good ones.*

~ t.

Dear New Dad,

We are a hot mess. My children are asking questions I don't know how to answer, things far above my pay grade. Come and relieve this constant pressure to throw a football. I cannot do this well.
> *Hurry, please.*

~ t.

Dear Love,

I prayed for you today. I am asking God to give you a spirit of wisdom and revelation, that you may know him better.
    Please find me soon.

                                        Love, Your Wife

Dear You,

I broke up with someone today. I broke up with him because I knew he wasn't you.

                                        Waiting,
                                        t.

The letters kept me focused on the one I was waiting for. They reminded me that this person was real, that this wait could be worth it. And they kept my decisions pure when I was, let's say, distracted. If I could write these letters to someone whom I believed really and truly existed, then I could save other things for him too.

When Peter and I met on a Tuesday night in Starbucks—when one cup of coffee turned into many more, and then coffee turned into dinner, which turned into meeting my children and my parents—the letters began to take on a different tone. I began to write a name at the top of those letters. I could write with a specific person in mind. After he asked me to marry him, I wrapped up the book and gave it to him.

I love remembering the night when we sat down to look at those pages together, when we began piecing together his time line and mine. We had been on parallel paths, living separate, single lives and drinking coffee in the same place at different hours of the same days. I had written the date on each letter, so we were able to align where we had each been. He had been lonely, or in jail, or in recovery. And though I did not know his name, his face, or his story, I had been praying him through, all along.

The beauty of these practices is the gift of noticing. To never stop looking is indeed a skill.

Tyler taught me this game he invented for whenever he's bored: his Noticing Game. When he's in the car on a long, familiar drive, or when he's waiting for me to finish a conversation so we can leave wherever he's finished being, he plays the Noticing Game. He looks around him, intent on finding something he's never seen before.

(It's a joy to raise an artist. He teaches me.)

Waiting is a time for noticing, and sometimes, in the long season of being separated from what we want, we discover that waiting is the only time we notice God.

God is in the in-between. Waiting for us to look for him differently. To notice him.

Look up. Look around. See.

Write it down.

· · ·

Keep a green tree in your heart and a singing bird may come.

CHINESE PROVERB

Above all, watch with glittering eyes the whole world around you because the greatest secrets are always hidden in the most unlikely places.

ROALD DAHL, *THE MINPINS*

CHAPTER 10

Stop Looking at the Clock
When Time Stands Still

My oldest son, Tucker, is in his first year of middle school as I write this, so he is navigating the brave new world of different classes, multiple teachers, locker combinations, and open seating in the cafeteria. There is a special place in my heart for middle schoolers. Everybody seems hungry all the time. Hungry and moody and exhausted. All that growing—physically, intellectually, and socially—can really take it out of a person. (And that person's parents.)

Tuck has been very fortunate to have had kind teachers all the way through elementary school. They have all loved him well, and he blossomed under their watchful eyes. So it came as a shock to him this year when he got the first teacher he didn't especially enjoy. We call her the Slow Talker. She has a slow pace to her instruction style, and I'm sure it resonates with some of her students. But it nearly drives Tuck to the brink. He cannot deal.

Each night at dinner—more accurately, on the one or two nights a week when we can eat dinner together, in between baseball practice, theater rehearsals, and youth-group events—we have a tradition that I like to call "High-Low." Everyone shares their high point and low moment of the day. Sometimes we call it Sunshine and Rain. The Best and the Rest. My sons like to call it Sugar and Booger. Or Happy and Crappy. Or Hearts and Farts.

(I may have mentioned that we are in the middle-school years.)

Tuck's low moments usually include the Slow Talker. How he's so frustrated. How her classroom is like a vortex for the passing of time. Nothing seems to happen for those forty-two minutes. The clock stands still. Time stops. Oh, the agony.

(I can relate. The same was true in tenth-grade Advanced Language Arts. It's a rite of passage, this tolerance of boredom in the classroom.)

You can perhaps imagine my surprise when Tucker's high came from a great discovery in the classroom of the Slow Talker. "Mom, the most amazing thing happened today. I discovered a way to make time go so much faster." He paused for emphasis. He made a circle with his fingers to illustrate the magnitude. He let the silence linger, as if to say, *Are you ready for this?* "Time goes so much faster when I don't stare at the clock."

Well, imagine that.

"Tell me more about this," I said.

I have learned that this is the absolute very best and safest response to the things my children are learning. It's my go-to for new information. Good, bad, alarming, surprising—this response works for all of the above.

- "Mom, I think I want to stop playing football."
  "Tell me more about this."

- "Mom, I want to invite a girl over for dinner."
  "Tell me more about this."

- "Mom, I know where to find marijuana in our neighborhood."
  "Tell me more about this."

- "Mom, today I learned the word *bisexual*."
  "Tell me more about this."

(Tuck it away, moms and dads. It's the Great Conversational Time Buyer.)

Thankfully, this was proving to be one of the easier topics to navigate. "Something happens when you don't stare at the clock? Tell me more about this."

"Well, today I decided to do my own experiment. Instead of looking at the clock, I paid attention to what the teacher was saying. I took notes and followed along in the book. I didn't look at the clock *at all*. And before I knew it, the bell rang. Class was over, Mom. I couldn't believe it. Weird, but it works."

(Actually, I remember discovering that very same thing in tenth-grade Advanced Language Arts. Weird, but it works.)

There is something about the art of distractions and the adage about the watched pot. When we obsess and perseverate over the passing of time, it all seems to go so much slower. This is especially true in the larger themes of life, when we are waiting for grander things than for a class to be over. When it becomes all you can think about, then impatience melds with sadness, depression, and, often, a heavy dose of self-absorption.

Think about it. When you want to be in a relationship, all you see around you is the coupling of the world, everyone paired off in groups of two. When you're waiting for a baby, all you notice is the sheer number of pregnant women at the park, the mall, the airport—*everywhere*. When you are looking for work, you can feel painfully aware of the gainfully employed.

When you are waiting for yes, all you hear is no.

Peter has taught me one of the three pillars of Alcoholics Anonymous: "Be of Service." When you are feeling sorry for yourself, get out and serve someone else. Look up. Look around. Other things are happening in the world that have nothing to do with you. Step into the action. Become a servant of something that is separate from your own interests. You'll be amazed at how much more there is to think about.

What could this look like for you while you wait? Maybe you could benefit from looking up. Look around. Look at the people around you.

Take a walk. Take a class. Take up a hobby. Take notice.

Choose a skill. Choose a topic. Choose a place to volunteer. Choose someone to serve.

It doesn't mean you stop waiting. It doesn't even mean you stop *wanting*.

It only means you can stop staring at the clock.

It's weird, but it works.

. . .

If you're waiting on God—do what waiters do: serve. Break free of your comfort zone and do something . . . help someone, pray for someone, serve someone, be the gift for someone.

ANN VOSKAMP[1]

How wonderful it is that nobody need wait a single moment before starting to improve the world.

ANNE FRANK

Each of you should use whatever gift you have received to serve others, as faithful stewards of God's grace in its various forms.

Be generous with the different things God gave you, passing them around so all get in on it: if words, let it be God's words; if help, let it be God's hearty help.

1 PETER 4:10, NIV, MSG

CHAPTER 11

Sparrows and a Tattoo
Build Your Altar

A few years ago, I was honored to accept an invitation to speak at a women's event in California. When I arrived at the airport, there was a delightful gaggle of women to greet me: the director of women's ministry, the lead pastor's wife, and a few of the key volunteers who were executing the event. (It takes a village to raise a child . . . and to effectively execute a women's-ministry event.)

They whisked me away to lunch at a beachside café. We chatted over lunch about important things, the things we love, the things that worry us, the things that keep us up at night. The realness of life. Skip the small talk, I say. Tell me who you really are. I'll do the same. Friendship was born immediately. How I love when that happens, when you meet someone for the first time and find an instant sisterhood that goes miles deep.

After lunch, they said, "Well, we have a few hours before the evening kicks off tonight, and we have a few ideas about what we could do next. We could take you to this wonderful gelato place that we love"—there was a pause here where they exchanged conspiratorial glances, and I swear their eyes sparkled—"or, we could get tattoos."

They looked at me, waiting, now that the big question was on the table. The anticipation was palpable as I weighed the options. I think they thought it would take me longer to decide.

"Sure! Let's do it," I said. "If ever there was a great day for a tattoo, this is that day."

And that's how I found myself at a beachfront tattoo parlor, getting inked with a bunch of women I had just met.

Yes, it was wonderful in the way of all spontaneous adventures. But the truth is, I had decided long before that moment that I wanted to get a tattoo. This was my second, and it's true what they say: Tattoos are just a touch addicting. So I had a plan. My new friends simply gave me an impromptu opportunity to follow through.

During my season of single parenting, I held deeply to the Bible's imagery of sparrows.

Even the sparrow finds a home,
    and the swallow builds her nest and raises her young
at a place near your altar,
    O Lord of Heaven's Armies, my King and my God![1]

Not a single sparrow can fall to the ground without your Father knowing it.[2]

What is the price of five sparrows—two copper coins? Yet God does not forget a single one of them.[3]

Don't be afraid; you are more valuable to God than a whole flock of sparrows.[4]

Couple these with one of my favorite lines from an old hymn, "His eye is on the sparrow, / And I know He watches me," and I had my tattoo chosen. Three sparrows, to represent me and my two young boys.

Some people say that if you're going to get a tattoo, you should *get a tattoo*. Make a statement with your body art. Go big or go home. But I didn't necessarily want my tattoo to exemplify everything I am about. Just one of the things I am about.

(Deeply about.)

So I looked through the artist's book of choices, and I found a whole flock of birds in flight, feminine and silhouetted. I chose three, and I climbed on the table, bared my left foot, and let him at it. Here is a good place to tell you that it hurt like three hundred bee stings. My other tattoo is on the inside of my right forearm, which, it turns out, is quite a bit fleshier than the top of my foot, which is seemingly all bones and tendons and nerve endings. Never have I been more thankful for three little sparrows, as opposed to the silhouette of a great peregrine falcon.

As it turns out, my new friends liked the birds-on-the-feet idea, and they each chose a sparrow of their own. The day took a wild and unexpected turn, not the least of which was the wardrobe change before I took the stage. (No, I would *not* like to put the bandaged, newly tattooed foot into high heels, thank you. And thank you, Lord, for cute flip-flops that one can even teach in.)

At last contact with my California friends, they were meeting regularly for beachside lunches and calling themselves The Sparrows. (Be still my heart.)

. . .

I do have another tattoo. On the inside of my right forearm, you'll find the word *betrothed*. As a bonus, it's in my own handwriting, as if I just inked it on with a Sharpie from inside my big brown bag. The other tattoo is important to me in a different way.

The week before Robb died, I was sitting in a coffee shop, typing away to finish many writing deadlines. I took a break and read my Bible for a little while, and I found this verse:

I will betroth you to me forever.[5]

I have to be honest, I had never read very much of Hosea before that moment. But on that night, this verse captivated me. Especially one word in particular: *betroth*.

I felt like God was trying to get my attention with that word. It gripped my thinking, and I thought of what (little) I knew about being betrothed. Basically, on a surface level, I knew it meant to be engaged to be married, to be pledged to someone. There were promises in that word, promises of hope and a future, of a beautiful plan for life together. In the corner of that coffee shop, I wrote a poem about that word, that verse, that idea. I am betrothed to the Lord. I am the bride of Jesus Christ. He loves me, he sees me, he knows me. I am betrothed.

I had that encounter on Monday night, and Robb died on Thursday morning. When I had written the poem, he wasn't even sick. One week later, as a heartbroken young widow delivering her husband's eulogy, I read it to those gathered at his funeral.

I realized I was right in what I felt in that coffee shop: Jesus had been trying to get my attention indeed. With that word, *betrothed*, he was whispering to me, "Tricia, we have a rough week in front of us. By the end of this week, you will not be a wife. But I need you to know that you will still be a bride. You are mine. I've got this, and I've got you."

And so, on what would have been our eleventh wedding anniversary, I got that word inked on my right arm. I chose that patch of canvas to remind me of another promise: He is the Lord, my God, who takes hold of *my right hand* and says, "Do not be afraid; I will help you."[6] I needed everything about those promises in the journey to come.

- *You are not alone. You are betrothed. Don't be afraid. He's got you.*

While I was doing research for this book, I learned another level to all of this. I was reading about when God instructed the Israelites to build the altar of sacrifice in the Tabernacle courtyard because he wanted a place to meet with them.[7] Throughout the Bible we see many different kinds of altars, and they are always an invitation to or a memorial of an encounter with God.[8] An altar is a place to remember an encounter, to recall forgiveness, to remember promises, to return to worship, and to return to pray.

When the Lord asked his people to build this altar in the entrance of the Tent of Meeting, he wanted them to create a place where they could "meet" with him. And when he offered that invitation, he intentionally used a specific word[9] that means *betroth*. I learned that the word *betrothed* comes from the root of a Greek word[10] that also means "to remember."

Stay with me as we round this corner: If we connect the dots in a full circle, the word written on my wrist means "meet me" and "remember." I can look at the dark ink, and I can meet God again and remember.

In some ways, my tattoos feel like an altar. An altar is a place to recall how we have been altered. They mark the turns in the journey, the places where God met us, the mornings after the long waits.

I wish I could tell you this was part of my plan all along

in choosing the sparrows and the word *betrothed*, but this knowledge knocked on my mind seven years after my first visit to the tattoo parlor. That kind of learning is true to the nature of the God who meets me where I am: He reveals himself in new ways, with new layers, on new mornings.

. . .

When Peter came into our lives, as the greatest answer to a prayer we had been most persistent about, Tyler looked down at my foot one day and said, "Mom, you have to get another bird. There are four of us now. Maybe you can get a big one to be at the front of the line, leading all the other birds."

As much as I deeply loved his sentiment and awareness, this tattoo is not meant to replicate our family in its many stages and forms. It represents a season, a very specific season of waiting and cocooning and learning to fly. A season of believing—of choosing to believe, despite outward appearances—that God had his eye on three sparrows who meant a great deal to him. He wouldn't let us out of his hand, his sight, or his care. And now, years later, when I encounter a season that calls everything I know into question, I can look down and recall. Our God is—was, and will be again—faithful.

When you're waiting on God, an altar gives you a place to meet and remember. It doesn't have to be tattooed onto your body; it can be written in your journal, represented in a pile of rocks in your home, or captured in a photo or a truth painted on a wall. An altar keeps you coming back. And the practice of returning reminds you of one thing most of all: He's there. He's got you.

. . .

Every hour of the light and dark is a miracle.
WALT WHITMAN, "MIRACLES"

We must be willing to let go of the life we have planned, so as to have the life that is waiting for us.
JOSEPH CAMPBELL

Reflections on Becoming

. . .

- Maybe all you can offer to the Lord is your honesty. Every emotion is safe with deference to a holy God. Tell him how you feel. Be honest about what you are afraid of.

- What questions do you have that begin with the word *when*? Write them all down.

- Remember that if you can't find your questions, you can find your voice, and if you can't find your praise, you can borrow from someone before you. Borrow their honesty and their words.

- When have you experienced the long wait of disease or death? Journal about that season. Are you walking near someone you love who is in a crisis of waiting? What effect has their journey had on your own heart? How can you best help that person not to feel alone? And if no helpful answers come to mind, it might not hurt to simply and thoughtfully . . . ask them what they need.

- When and how have you sensed God's presence in a wait? When have you *not* felt his presence? What emotions did you feel, or what questions did you want to ask him?

- Do you recognize possible symptoms of depression in your mind and heart? Talk with someone you trust, or seek a pastor or counselor who can advise you. You don't have to go it alone.

- Ask Jesus to show you a glimpse of hope. Ask him to show you where he is. Give him the honesty of your broken pieces. Ask him to give you himself. Prepare yourself to find him in the middle of your wait.

- Think of an altar you can create as you recall this season of waiting. Build a reminder of when you waited, of how God met you in the journey and in the waiting. Build your altar.

- Have you felt angry at God when no answer comes? He already knows your emotions; take the time to write or say them. Have the hard conversations with God—he is big enough to receive them. Read one of the suggested psalms or find another that seems to say what you feel. Use the psalmist's words to help you find your own, and journal your emotions as David did, as questions and prayers to God.

- With just three or four 3 × 5 cards, write out one Bible verse per card that has a truth you want to remember, one of God's promises for the season where you find yourself. Try the steps suggested for keeping those verses purposefully in your mind.

- Keep a simple journal of the circumstances or thoughts in which those verses came to mind when you weren't trying to focus on them. What might God be doing in your heart through his Word?

PART THREE

Awakening

Sleep never came easy for Peter while he was in jail. That nightly insomnia was hard to face. After a day of work, he'd bring back one melatonin, a natural sleep aid, and would swallow it just before he began the check-in process. The pill took the edge off his wakefulness and gave him a narrow window to fall asleep. Anything to help him get through the night.

But one night, upon his reentry, a new guard was on duty to check him back in. He began the pat-down before Peter had taken the melatonin. When the guard felt the melatonin tablets in the pocket of Peter's shirt, he snapped to protocol. "What is this?"

"Melatonin. It helps me sleep."

And then, as Peter says, "Everything got serious in a hurry." With no further questioning, the officer put cuffs on Peter. Two more guards appeared by his side, and they escorted him to isolation and locked him in until further notice. They left Peter swimming in his thoughts and unsure what had just happened until he was hauled to an investigation room for questioning.

"What was that pill you tried to bring in?"

"Melatonin, sir. It helps me sleep."

"It's contraband."

"No, sir, another guard said it was okay. I've been taking it every night when I arrive. I have permission. I've been doing this for weeks."

"That's impossible and untrue. You signed a paper saying you wouldn't bring in any outside drugs for personal use or distribution, and you broke that agreement."

Suddenly he was being accused of bringing contraband for distribution inside the jail, selling it to other inmates, and that meant he would be charged with a *felony*. Peter tried to explain where he had bought it, where they could find it on grocery-store shelves, that he had brought only enough for himself, and that he had permission from another guard, but none of his facts could be verified. The captain gave him a logbook filled with pictures of officers, asking him to identify the two who had given him permission to take a pill upon his reentry. The pictures were all taken on the officers' first day on duty, and some were decades old. Peter said it was like looking at a retiree's high-school yearbook photo, and he made his best estimate on what those officers must have looked like years ago, based on pages and pages of choices. But he felt hopeless. No guard would confess to this, and none of them would tell on another for breaking a rule.

They let him make one phone call: to his lawyer.

Peter had thought that his first night in jail—sleeping on the floor in a straitjacket—was the most horrible night of his life, but this night alone in isolation was even worse. He said, "I thought being stripped naked was the worst thing that could happen to me. But this night of waiting, with the looming possibility of a federal offense, the threat of being sent to a federal penitentiary for a year or longer, all because I had been foolish enough to break the rules for a sleeping pill? The panic was pure and crippling. The night was endless."

As he lay on his cement bed, in the depths of emotional and physical darkness, Peter still vividly remembers what happened next—and always will: A thick darkness filled the room, and he heard a voice say, "You're not getting out of this. You're going down. This is the end for you."

He was sure this was the voice of Satan or one of his messengers. It was not in his imagination; that voice was in the room, so close to him. It was not of this world. He broke down, weeping in terror. He lay with his face to the floor, and he reached for his only personal belonging in the room: his Bible. He flipped through the pages, frantically looking for anything to help him, any truth to cling to. By the light from the hallway, Peter opened to Mark 11: "If you believe I can throw a mountain into the sea, and if you don't doubt, then you can ask for anything."[1] He read the words again and again, pleading through the night.

Please, God. Please.

Please.

The next morning, an officer came to retrieve Peter from his isolation cell. "You have a phone call." The officer escorted him to a private room to take the call, and there were three of his sisters on a video screen from a police station across town. Peter told me, "I didn't even want to look at them. I was so ashamed. Who gets in trouble while they're in jail? How foolish could I have been? I had to tell them I didn't know if I'd get out. Then I faced seeing their sadness. Their faces. They were trying to be strong for me, but their beloved baby brother was now in jail facing federal charges. I didn't know when I'd even see them again, and I only had myself to blame."

The captain interrupted the call. "When you're finished, I need to speak with you." Peter said good-bye to his sisters with great trepidation. This was it. He was moments away from being transferred to federal prison in Cañon City. He approached the captain with all the courage he could find, bracing himself for the inevitable.

"Listen," the captain said, "we talked to the officers you identified, *and they admitted they had seen that pill.* We've had a breach in protocol. We are very sorry for the confusion, and every federal charge has been dropped."

What????

Peter could not believe the captain's words. The potential emotional relief was hard to wrap his mind around; it seemed too good to be true.

Two realities crashed into one another:

"If you believe I can throw a mountain into the sea, and if you don't doubt, then you can ask for anything."

And "Every federal charge has been dropped."

Tears ran down Peter's face as he told me what happened next: He ran—full speed—back to his cell. "I dropped to my knees," he recalled, "and I thanked him. I thanked my God for a miracle. For setting me free. I was *free.*"

Peter would still have to finish his sentence with work release, but he would not face federal prison.

His freedom was tangible.

The end was in sight.

. . .

As Peter and I talked about his encounter with the heavy voice in the darkness of his cell on that long night, another possibility brought a whole different perspective to light. He had always thought his encounter was with a messenger from Satan to tell him his fate, that the end of his life was near. And that seemed plausible.

But what if—just *what if*—his encounter was with an angel of the Lord? Or what if he had encountered the Lord himself?

In Genesis 32, the night before Jacob would face his brother—the brother who wanted to kill him—Jacob felt uncertain about how it would go. And he found himself alone in the dark night of the desert, where he suddenly had to wrestle with "a man." A physical battle ensued between the two. Jacob would not let that man overpower him, and he also would not let the man go. Jacob wrestled with him until daybreak. And throughout the hours of that long, dark night, as Jacob wrestled with the unknown man, I imagine that he also wrestled with his understanding of who he was. I don't think it's a far stretch to imagine that he wrestled mentally with his relationships, what he was afraid of, what he held tightly to, what he hadn't been willing to let go of. And I imagine he wrestled with a good measure of his pride. He could not have guessed that he was wrestling with the God of creation, the God who held his future in those very hands.

When the sun came up, Jacob had had an encounter that changed him forever—and left him with a limp. As my pastor has pointed out, Jacob would still face his brother the next morning, but without his strength and pride. Jacob met Esau as a broken man.

It reminds me of when Peter or I have engaged in a battle of wills with one of our sons. Sometimes, one of the boys will lock horns with an alarming dose of bullheadedness, and he needs someone stronger than him to say, "You *will not* win this. Fight as long as you want to, but you *are* going down." It takes a loving parent to engage the fight, no matter how stubborn the young fighter, and win.

Peter's wrestling match was not physical that night, but he'd heard that voice as clearly as if the man was standing over him as he lay there prostrate on the floor. The voice was real; he heard it. Who was that man? Was it a messenger of Satan sent to destroy his hope for good? Or could it have been God having the final battle of wills with Peter's stubborn heart? Saving him for *good*?

. . .

Peter's journey began with eleven months of waiting for sentencing after his third DUI. He waited forty-eight hours to learn his fate with federal charges—though that wait felt more like a decade. He waited thirty-eight years to be delivered from his addiction to alcohol and to be released from the prison of his own mind, from his belief that he was only funny, fun, and worthy of love when he was inebriated and performing. He waited through the consequences of his own decisions. He waited for an awakening, for a new chance.

CHAPTER 12

A Game of Catch, a Lavender Shirt, and Root Beer Floats

Waiting for Jesus

"Hey, Mom? Can you come up and talk to me?" Tuck asks this every night. After the TV, the snacks, the brushing teeth, the bedtime meds, the hugs, the kisses, and the bedtime prayers, he asks for time with me. He is in the latest years of childhood, almost taller than me, and his thoughts come alive at bedtime. This routine that should be so precious and intentional comes at the point of my day when I am poured out. That is the most frustrating thing about bedtime: It comes at the *end* of the day. I'm always so worn out by then. When I've just crossed the finish line, my son presents me with one more request.

I go up to his room, navigating the steep stairs that are always littered with Legos, shoes, and dog toys. "What's up, pal?"

"I just love you so much." This is how he always begins

our bedtime chats. And it's not a bad start. This makes the trek upstairs worth every step. He lies in his bed and reaches his arms for me to hug him. I lean down to him, so we are nose to nose.

"I love you too, buddy. Anything else you need tonight?"

"I feel far from God."

Tucker's thoughts are deepest at this hour. This is when he processes concepts like gravity, time, eternity, and justice. Tonight, his heart is tackling spiritual intimacy.

"Tell me more about that."

"Well, when our pastor says we should close our eyes and go into the throne room of God, and we are just supposed to walk up to him, I'm always like, *What? How do I do that? What does that even mean?*"

I know just what he means. We have a pastor whose prayers are so very dear and intimate. When she leads us in corporate prayer together, she always asks us to picture entering the throne room with Jesus, and she invites us to imagine what that is, where it is, what it looks like. Krissy says, "Maybe it's an open field at your favorite park. Maybe it's a cabin where you vacation. Maybe it's under a blanket of stars. Maybe you've pictured a large cathedral with a throne, front and center, where you can approach the throne of grace with confidence."

For a person with a mind that thinks quite literally, these metaphors could be a big leap. I explain, "Well, Tuck, that's really just a prayer exercise that invites you to use your imagination. You can picture anything you want. There is no right or wrong answer. It's about taking your mind wherever you feel closest to God."

"Where do you go?"

"Well, it might sound silly, but my place is the corner table at Starbucks. That's where Jesus meets me."

We have this place, Jesus and I. We met there every day for two years, when I was learning to think and breathe and talk to him again. And when I close my eyes to think of intimacy with Jesus, I go there in my mind. It's the same Starbucks, but it has been transformed into a most beautiful and inviting space for two. The restaurant is always empty except for our table and two chairs, and the room is always filled with white candles, lit and sparkling.

In my imagination, Jesus always wears a lavender shirt for our dates together. He wears great jeans with a sharp leather belt. Beautiful Oxford shoes and that lavender dress shirt, tucked in. I've always had a thing for a man in lavender, and Jesus dresses up to meet me for coffee. He looks so handsome, this Jesus of mine.

When I enter the throne room, Jesus is delighted every single time. His face lights up. He invites me to sit with him, to tell him everything. He wants to know what I am thinking about. What I am learning. What I am worried about. What I need. What I delight in. What I am working on. What I am creating. I love that he's never bored, and he never asks me to hurry up or just give him the headlines. He always wants to know. From across the table, he holds my right hand between both of his as we talk.

"Where does Peter go in his mind to meet with Jesus?"

"Peter has told me he goes to Argyle"—the name of the sprawling family grounds where we sat on the rocking chairs together. "That's where he meets God, and that's how he imagines heaven too."

Tucker looks at me, and then he looks up at the ceiling. "I don't know where my place is."

"How about the baseball field? Could you imagine meeting Jesus there? You could play catch."

I can see that this imagery is working for him. I take a few more steps in that direction.

"Imagine that, Tucker. Imagine walking to the field. Imagine Jesus handing you a glove. Maybe he says, 'Here you go, Tuck. Let's play. Tell me what's on your mind.'"

Tucker smiles. "His ball would land in the mitt every time, Mom. Because he would have all the power."

"And maybe yours would, too, since he would share his power with you. That's how it goes when you choose to spend time with him. You can do things you could never do on your own."

There is silence. And then Tuck says, "It's easier to imagine playing that game of catch with my first dad."

"I get that, buddy. That's because we have memories of him. We know what he looks like. We know how his voice sounds, and we know what his laughter sounds like. So it's easier to imagine being with him."

"Why didn't you have me sooner?"

"What do you mean?"

"Why wasn't I born earlier?"

I know where he's going with this—he wants to know why he didn't get more life with his dad. He thinks an earlier start would have made a difference, given him more time. Maybe it would have.

"I was too young to be a mom."

"You got married when you were twenty, and I was born when you were twenty-five. Why did it take so long?"

I piece together a true explanation about finishing college, starting my job, moving across the country, and growing up a little more. I toss in a few words of wisdom about how fun it is to be newlyweds for a while before inviting a baby into the family.

He says, "I just have so many questions."

Me too, sweet boy.

"What would you like to know?"

"They're not questions for you. They're for God."

"What would you like to ask him?"

"I want to ask, 'Why my family? Why my dad? Why did he only give me five years with him?'"

This is the evolving truth about childhood trauma. When a child loses a parent so early in life, their grief grows and changes with time. He grieves Robb every time he experiences a new life stage, a new accomplishment, a new milestone. Tuck has to miss his dad all over again.

"I have asked all those same questions, Tuck. And they're all valid. One of the things I love about God is that he lets us ask our questions. We won't know some of those answers until we can ask God ourselves someday. Maybe you can ask him during that game of catch you'll get to play."

I wait in his silence, waiting for the next question.

"Mom, can you send Dad up? I mean, no offense, but I just want to see if his views match yours."

Offended? Not even a little. More like relieved to share the load. Thankful for this New Dad to whom I can pass the baton. Happy to let him take a shift at answering the great questions of the young theologian.

I picture Peter downstairs, watching this week of play-off baseball games while his team is in the lead for the World Series. I lean over to kiss Tucker's forehead, one more time. "I'll send him up after this inning."

"Love you so much, Mom."

"And I love you forever, pal."

. . .

Every year on Robb's birthday, we go to Red Robin for dinner. Because, Bottomless Root Beer Floats. Last year, Peter was away for the weekend at a men's conference, so there were only three of us at the table. It felt a little too much like the lonely days.

(That feels like it should be capitalized. Like a month or a whole time period: January, the Jurassic Period, the Lonely Days.)

"We're here to celebrate," I told the waiter.

"Oh, is it a birthday?"

"It is. A very special one."

Tuck pointed to the empty spot. "Our first dad died, and root beer floats were his favorite. So we need three root beer floats, please."

Our waiter was maybe twenty-two years old. And he handled it so well. "I respect that so much, man. I'm so glad you're here. Three root beer floats coming up."

Did I mention they were bottomless? On their fourth serving, I said, "Guys, please pay attention to what your bodies may be telling you right now. I'd love to not have anybody sick."

Tucker looked dreamily into his tall glass. "I bet my first dad is having root beer floats tonight. So many. When I get to heaven, I'm going to drink root beer floats all day long with him. And we'll never get sick."

"I love that idea," I said. "Do you ever miss him anymore?"

"Sometimes, but I don't really feel like I have to since I have my new dad." He pointed again to the empty chair. Perhaps it was more accurately the Dad Chair.

"Buddy, I feel exactly the same way. Exactly."

We made a list of the ways the dads are different. Because it's good to do that sometimes, to remember we are thankful for both, and to feel the freedom to love them differently. Root beer floats help us remember.

Meals are like that; they invite us to remember. The senses of taste and smell are packed with memories, and they're emotional memories that don't fade with time. One whiff of this scent, one sip of that flavor, and we can find ourselves whisked back to another time and place, remembering a person who has been gone a long time.

I think this is why Jesus chose to eat with his friends on the last night before he would be captured and killed. He knew what was coming, and he wanted to solidify a message and a memory. He shared with them the bread, then the wine. He asked them to take, eat, drink, and remember. This same one who created our senses of taste and smell and our capacity for memory wove them all together in a tradition that would lead us to remember.

I've attended many churches throughout my life, and I've received Communion in many ways. Sometimes we have filed out of our pew and approached a table where we take a hunk of bread and dip it into a chalice of grape juice or wine. Sometimes we have come forward to receive a cracker and a cup of juice from the pastor standing at the front, below the cross. Sometimes we have stayed in our seats while ushers pass trays down the row, trays that are still cold from the church-kitchen refrigerator. (Anytime the tray comes down the row, I must confess: I feel a surge of Communion anxiety because I absolutely do not want to be the one to drop the metal tray of cups and juice and crackers. And I never have. Yet the possibility always exists.)

Sometimes, I'm thoughtfully engaged. Sometimes, I am distracted and bored. One time, my sons found a whole tray of leftover Communion servings in the back of the sanctuary, and they started throwing them back like they were doing tequila shots. (That was a winning moment for me, as a mom. Some of the church ladies are still recovering from that image.) I'm telling you, the practice of Communion and I have a long history together.

Some people believe that the bread and wine have no spiritual significance, that the elements are as powerless as toast and orange juice. Other people believe that this Eucharist is the actual blood from Jesus' veins and the actual flesh from his body, broken for us. But the truth is, regardless of where you land on that spectrum of theology, Jesus asked us to eat the bread and drink the wine as a way of remembering him. The bread reminds us that he was a man, and he had a body. He was here. He walked the earth, felt our pain, ate our food, and cried over the things that broke our hearts. The wine is a symbol that his body was nailed to a cross, his blood was poured out, and he died carrying the full weight of our sins, so we wouldn't have to. He asked us to regularly eat and drink and remember his sacrifice.

Can you imagine how odd our present-day Communion practices might have seemed to members of the early church? The first ones to claim the name of Jesus, the ones who received the letters Paul wrote, the ones who were loved by Peter or John? Imagine if they could have traveled in time to see us and the way we do it, filing forward or passing trays down the pews, with a crumb of cracker and a tablespoon of juice. It's so different from how they experienced Communion! I picture them sitting around someone's table, grabbing a hunk of bread and holding their own cups of wine, sharing stories about Jesus. They're laughing as they remember together, consoling each other when they miss him terribly. And they're passionately reminding each other to never, ever forget. *Always remember that he was here, the Son of God, with us. And always remember: He said he'll come back.* Someone raises a glass. *Eat. Drink. Remember.*

So, when I think about the tradition that my sons and I have, the Bottomless Root Beer Floats? Well, as silly as it sounds, it feels kind of like a sacred tradition. It's not that different from the juice and the cracker, the wine and the bread, the blood and the body of Christ. Maybe it's silly. But somehow, the whole thing makes sense to us. Sometimes theology is like that: It's a delicious parallel waiting in the glass in front of me.

Jesus is someone we wait for, but he is already with us now. We wait, but also we don't have to. We can meet him then, but we can know him now. We live in the midst of the longing and the awakening all at once.

We drink, and we remember. He was here. And we'll see him again. And this is only a taste of how great it will be.

I wonder often what that throne room will really look like. Maybe I've been off base all along, or maybe I'll get there and find that he has indeed created a place just for me. In all the miles and acres of heaven, maybe there's a coffee shop with white candles and a corner table in a space that's all our own.

I cannot wait to see him there. I hope he wears the lavender shirt.

. . .

Christians are people who wait. We live in liminal time, in the already and not yet. Christ has come, and he will come again. We dwell in the meantime. We wait.

TISH HARRISON WARREN, *LITURGY OF THE ORDINARY*

Now we see only a reflection as in a mirror; then we shall see face to face. Now I know in part; then I shall know fully, even as I am fully known.

1 CORINTHIANS 13:12, NIV

CHAPTER 13

Seeds in the Ground, Butterfly in the Cocoon

The Gifts of Waiting

When my boys were small, I got us a little family of cater-pillars and a butterfly garden. We made a little habitat with leaves and twigs, we fed them sugar water, and we named each one. We checked on them first thing in the morning, and we said good-night to them before we went up the stairs at the end of the day. They were more than a science project; they were little tiny pets. For a few weeks, they were part of our family.

In those weeks of hosting the butterfly garden in my kitchen, I read *Hope for the Flowers*, a darling book by Trina Paulus. It's the sweet story of Stripe and Yellow, two cater-pillars who become butterflies. In the book, Yellow sees another caterpillar spinning a cocoon, and he asks, "If I decide to become a butterfly, . . . what do I do?"

And the other caterpillar replies, "Watch me. I'm making a cocoon. It looks like I'm hiding, I know, but a cocoon is no escape. It's an in-between house where the change takes place. . . . During the change, it will seem . . . that nothing is happening—but the butterfly is already becoming. It just takes time!"[1]

Some waits force us into a personal cocoon. We have to huddle, accept the rest, and lean into the immobility of a process we can't yet see an end to. This kind of waiting can be an in-between place, a silent, withdrawn dwelling of growing and learning and changing. It is terrible and long and diffi-cult, but it is not something to cure. We can choose to fight it, ignore it, and delay it, but we may be resisting our chance to hide away for a while, to become something more beautiful than ever. Finding the gifts in the waiting takes time; there are no shortcuts.

When the need to wait shows up, especially if I wasn't expecting to wait, I'm not usually exactly thrilled. Especially if the wait has arrived on the wings of a broken heart. None of us want to suffer through spiritual, emotional, or physi-cal hardships, but such milestones rarely ask our permission. Maybe it's like lifting the silver lid on a platter, only to see all the things we never wanted, seemingly presented as a gift. We may find ourselves thinking, *I didn't ask for this, but it seems to be definitely mine.* We can refuse the gift we didn't ask for, or we can see what beauty might be waiting for us in the journey of the wait. After all, a cocoon doesn't stay a cocoon forever. Something is happening right now, because something new is waiting on the other side.

. . .

After the years of the great sadness, with no shortcuts, finally the season came when the sun began to shine in my spirit, when I could leave the house without anxiety again, when I felt a sense of solid ground beneath my feet again. It was time to come out of the cocoon and stretch my wings. A new wait began: the wait for the New Dad.

My children's prayers were so fervent and so literal. They worried that I would fall in love with someone who didn't love God, or who couldn't love my children, or who only spoke Spanish. They thought the Lord would bring him to our front door, like Publishers Clearing House.

When a repairman came to work on our alarm system, my son pulled me by the sleeve into the kitchen to whisper, "Mommy, do you think that's him?"

"Do I think that's who?"

"The New Dad."

"Him? No. No, I do not."

When I walked hastily past a salesman at the mall, and when I was maybe a tiny bit rude to him for asking twice for a moment of my time, my children scolded me for being so harsh and unapproachable. After all, maybe the question he wanted to ask me was if I would have dinner with him and become his wife and travel the world with him. No, my loves. He wanted me to try a sample of his skin exfoliator. Mommy isn't interested. A girl doesn't exfoliate for just anybody.

And so, I didn't tell my children, but I quietly put myself on a ten-year plan. I would "simply" get these boys raised, and then I would see what life held for me in the department of love. I had learned that dating as a single parent was a whole different ball game, and it was distracting and emotionally exhausting—and that's when it was going *well*. I couldn't afford to be distracted. As I said often, I'd rather do it alone than do it wrong.

Meanwhile, my sons were growing taller. They longed for a dad. Their questions were growing out of my league and above my pay grade. I am a nurturer, and I was learning that you can't nurture a boy into manhood. A boy needs someone to call him out of safety and into courage. A boy needs someone who can see what he is capable of and expect him to do it—not protect him from it. A boy needs someone to let him play with matches and explore with power tools. A boy needs someone to model for him how to respect a woman. A boy needs someone to call him a man. Still, I wasn't willing to let just anybody into our world, no matter how sincerely my children believed anyone could do the job.

But then along came Peter. A best friend to my heart and a companion to my weary soul. He made me laugh harder than I ever had before, and certainly more often. He began to lift the world off my shoulders, and he offered to carry it with me. He threw a football with Tucker, he introduced us to the world of baseball, and he explained that there are athletes in the world who play more than one sport. He built Lego masterpieces with Tyler and coached him as a young actor, teaching him accents and dialogue. They acted alongside each other as the conductor and the boy hero in a local production of *The Polar Express*. On the morning Peter asked me to marry him, we visited the boys' school to take this good news right into their classrooms. After all, a ring for me was a promise to all three of us.

Peter was not our salvation. No person ever could be, ever should be, except for the Son of God. So when I say the Lord rescued us, it wasn't with Peter. But he rescued us from the darkness and hopelessness through the hope he gave us, and on that fertile soil, he planted the life of a new marriage.

In the darkness of the cocoon, I could not see anything except what was happening directly to me. Or more accurately, sometimes I could not see anything at all. I could only *feel*. I wonder if that's how it is for caterpillars, too. Unlike us, with our many seasons of life, caterpillars get one round in the cocoon, one chance to grow into a butterfly. So this cocoon situation is an unknown space for them. It's not like they're returning to familiar territory. Except for instinct, they don't know what's going on. They don't know what is happening, what they are becoming, or even *that* they are becoming. Perhaps they can't see it; they can only feel it.

For a long time, I could not see the sunshine, happiness, or hope. I could not see where God was, so it was easy for me to believe he wasn't in this at all. But, oh, how deceptive is the wait. I couldn't have been more wrong. Not only was he present but he was deeply in the details, weaving together four essential pieces:

1. The story God has been writing since the beginning of time.
2. Peter's story.
3. My story.
4. The story we could write together.

I couldn't know that then. And if you're in the cocoon right now, you probably find it hard to believe as well. Yes, the cocoon can be a beautiful place of growing, learning, and changing, but it's also a lonely, hungry place. It's not until later that we can see what was happening all along, what the Creator has been doing behind the scenes.

. . .

What are you hungry for? I don't mean food, necessarily; I mean a longing that's so deep, it's almost painful to name it. Maybe you long for a child. You long to be a parent. Maybe you are hungry for marriage—or for healing in the one you have. Maybe you long for physical relief from a difficult diagnosis. You are waiting, you are longing, and you are starved with hunger.

Maybe you are simply waiting for joy. You are weary of walking under a dark cloud and the heavy blanket of depression. You long for happiness and you're hungry for laughter.

Please hear me on this: I get that. I understand you. I will not say I know how you feel, but I may have been painfully close to where you stand. Can I show you what shined a little light into my dark cocoon?

Look at these verses with me:

> God blesses you who are hungry now,
>   for you will be satisfied.
> God blesses you who weep now,
>   for in due time you will laugh.[2]

This is not poetry. It is a promise. He promises that those who are hungry now will not always be. Those who are sad will one day laugh again. Not just smile, you guys. *Laugh.* Now, with that promise in your hands, couple it with this one, this passage for "after the waiting":

> Yes, the LORD has done amazing things for us!
>   What joy! . . .
> Those who plant in tears
>   will harvest with shouts of joy.[3]

> Those who go out weeping,
>   carrying seed to sow,
> will return with songs of joy.[4]

It says if you "*plant* in tears." It does not say if you "*are* in tears."

There is a subtle and very important difference there. Crying in itself does not guarantee forthcoming joy. Tears alone do not promise healing and laughter to come. The promise lives in the willingness to *plant* while you are in tears.

What does that mean, though? What are we to sow? How are we to plant?

We sow seeds each time we are honest in our conversations with the Lord. Each time we open ourselves to the vulnerability of intimacy, by saying what we really mean instead of an empty platitude. Are you so angry that you fear what you might do next? Tell him. Are you so discouraged you don't feel you can go another day? Tell him. Are you so weary that one more step feels like it will break you? Tell him. He already knows how we feel, and healing comes when we are honest about it. As we bring our brokenness, as we choose to believe he is in this journey and he is faithful, we are planting seeds.

Also, we sow seeds when we believe the truth of the words of Scripture. We can plant it by believing it, claiming it, and holding onto it with both hands. When you are in a season so dark that you cannot see the path before you, when your tears are so thick that you feel like you may drown, you can sow seeds by claiming one verse at a time.

These are some of the truths that I held on to in my darkest hours:

This I know: God is on my side![5]

My heart is confident in you, O God;
    my heart is confident.
No wonder I can sing your praises![6]

You came near when I called you,
    and you said, "Do not fear."[7]

Let my soul be at rest again,
    for the LORD has been good to me.[8]

For I know the one in whom I trust.[9]

You may have a hurt that will never, ever be healed in this lifetime, and I will never minimize the longing that feels like it could break you in two before this life is through. Don't put your tears away. While you are in the darkness, while you are waiting, plant seeds with your tears. Be honest with the Lord. Let them pour. Let them go. Trust the Lord to keep them, just as he promised. When we give him our tears, not a single one is wasted. He will restore you. He is faithful. His loving-kindness will never end. He is for you. And he is on your side. He longs to hear you laugh again too. And I know this: Laughter is never sweeter than after you've been sad.

Those who weep now will laugh.

Don't let this time be wasted.

Sow your seeds.

. . .

He did rescue us . . . and he will rescue us again.
We have placed our confidence in him, and he will
continue to rescue us.

2 CORINTHIANS 1:10

Don't turn away. Keep your gaze on the bandaged
place. That's where the light enters you.

RUMI

CHAPTER 14

The Answer We Don't Want
Still Waiting

I love family movie night. I love the coziness and the blankets
and the together of it all. It's one thing I think we do well.
Generally.

Last weekend, we decided to watch *Miracles from Heaven*.
Because how can you go wrong with Jennifer Garner?

It's based on a true story about Anna Beam, a little girl
with a rare, incurable disorder that keeps her from digesting
food. Her mom moves heaven and earth to get answers for her
daughter's symptoms, and her fierce mothering is relentless
and awesome. They can't find any answers, and they despair
that she'll probably die from this, when it all changes in an
instant. Anna falls three stories into a hollow tree, sustains a
life-threatening head injury, and then baffles her family with

(a) stories of her trip to heaven, and (b) signs of recovery from her fatal illness. In the end, Anna isn't at all surprised that she's healed, because God said she would be when he talked with her. She had told him she only wanted to go back if she was cured, and he promised her she would be. And here she was, cured indeed.

I kept checking my emotional barometer as we watched, analyzing how I felt about this story of miraculous healing. Stories like this generally don't rest well with me, not because I don't believe God can or would heal, but just that he didn't do that for my family. But it appeared, as I continued to check the pulse of my own reaction, that enough time has passed. Enough healing has come. It's not quite the tender wound it once was, this question about why God didn't do that for us. I like the story he has written into our new chapter, so it doesn't feel so white-hot painful.

But I didn't think about how this story would rest with my son.

I've said it before, and it continues to be true: When a child experiences deep loss at a young age, their under-standing changes with their cognitive growth. As they learn more about life, they experience more about death. As they grow and receive, they learn more about what they've lost. My children show me in their own ways when we have entered a new place, when the questions are new and the pain is fresh.

The movie finished, we turned up the lights, and I said, "Well, that was a good movie."

And my son said, "I've never been more angry in my life."

Oh. Oh, I see what has happened.

Okay, God. Go here with me. This is your territory.

Peter is so wise in situations like this, and he knows the boys feel a tension in having to protect his emotions while they process their own. After all, how can they miss their first dad if they're thankful for the one they have now? It's all so complicated, and he helps them navigate it by simply stepping back. He reminds them that their emotions are okay, his identity is secure, and they can feel how they feel and ask what they need. (And he often reminds them that he, too, would love to see his own dad again, given the choice.)

Just before he left the couch, Peter turned to me and said, "Help him to identify the difference between *angry* and *confused.*" Brilliant advice; just what I needed. And then Peter exited stage left.

I said, "Buddy, you said you feel angry, but I wonder if you feel confused."

"Yes. Yes! Confused! I feel angry and confused. Mom, why did God heal her? Does he love her more than he loves my dad?"

God, show me what to say.

And so we forged our way into dark waters where you can't see the bottom. He voiced his questions about why God heals some people and not others, particularly not our person.

I told him that I don't think God sends illnesses, but sometimes he lets them happen. I told him that I think God healed that little girl so he could remind the world that he can, but he didn't heal Robb because he was telling a different kind of story, a different kind of miracle, about how he is with us in our darkest hour.

He asked why God tests us.

I told him I don't believe God tests us, but the world does.

He asked why, if God has already won the war, does he let Satan keep winning battles? I told him I think God's giving the world time to believe him. I told him I think God has marked his calendar, and he's going to show up to wrap this thing up when he's ready. But the clock is ticking, and it won't always be this way.

He apologized for asking hard questions.

I told him I love his hard questions.

I promised him to always tell him what I know, and I asked him to be patient with me and with God when the answer is "I don't know."

I told him that it's in those gaps, in the space between questions and answers, where faith steps in.

I didn't give him any answers he wanted. But I gave him what I had. He didn't feel better, but he felt heard.

It's one thing to battle my own faith crises. It's a whole different something to trust God with my son's faith crises, to trust him to be enough.

But that's where faith steps in.

.   .   .

Probably one of my favorite people in the Bible is the persistent widow. I can't wait to meet her. I do realize there's a chance she's not a real person since she was a character in one of Jesus' stories, but still. I like her. In the parable that tells her story,[1] we don't get to know what injustice she was fighting for, but she would not take no for an answer. She kept showing up to the judge's house, day after day, asking and asking. I mean, the lady straight up *would not quit.*

Persistent can mean *dedicated, determined, patient, steadfast,* and *faithful.* But the less flattering synonyms include *bullheaded, stubborn, headstrong,* and *hell-bent.*[2] I might also add *crazy.* It's clear: She was not going to back down. The judge knew she would keep showing up until one of two things happened: (a) he gave her what she wanted, or (b) she died.

One version says, "For some time he refused. But finally he said to himself, 'Even though I don't fear God or care what people think, yet because this widow keeps bothering me, I will see that she gets justice, so that she won't eventually come and attack me!'"[3] I mean, come on. You have to hand it to a woman who gets results like that.

The whole point of that parable is to show the potential outcome for those with persistent faith, the answers for those who keep asking. Jesus told the story to prove that God's motives are far better than those of an unjust judge, and he is generous to say yes when we keep asking. He invites us to pray and not lose heart.

I leaned hard into this in my own years as a persistent widow, as I began asking God for big things. I've told you about that journal where I have pages of names, needs, and events, and circles upon circles, that I continue bringing to God every day. Even this morning, I prayed through each one of those, drawing a new line around each question I'm still asking. He may say yes; he may say no. But if God says no, I don't want it to be because I stopped asking. So I keep asking.

But let me be honest about the other side of that. While I feel confident in verses that call me to "pray without ceasing,"[4] I bristle at words like, "Your faith has healed you."[5] Those are harder for me to hold.

I have always had a problem with the complicated theology of faith healing. And *problem* doesn't feel like the right word. That conveys a need to air my grievances, to call a meeting with the people involved to discuss the matter at hand. That's not what I mean. I don't have any desire to debate someone's miracle with them. When God says yes, it's a reason to celebrate, not a reason to argue.

It's just that when you've seen the actual color of death on the face of someone you love, when you've known the absence of their spirit in this world, and when it's all too much too soon and it could have been avoided, it affects how you understand the stories of a God who gives and takes away.

So when I say I have a problem, it's more like a clenching in my spirit. My Grams would call it a "stitch in your side," that fleeting pain that I'd get in my ribs when I ran too hard as a child. The parallels are many. It's that kind of pain, from running hard, from exertion. It doesn't last forever, but it doesn't sit well. It feels like a pinch in my spirit that says, "What am I to do with this? Why is God willing to heal other people? Why does he say yes to them? Why couldn't I have that favor when I needed it most?"

I look at stories of Jesus healing people, and I wonder about their faith, how it was different from mine—or was it different at all? I wonder about Jesus' willingness and how he makes his decisions. Look at this story Luke told:

In one of the villages, Jesus met a man with an advanced case of leprosy. When the man saw Jesus, he bowed with his face to the ground, begging to be healed. "Lord," he said, "if you are willing, you can heal me and make me clean."

Jesus reached out and touched him. "I am willing," he said. "Be healed!" And instantly the leprosy disappeared.[6]

There it is again, the stitch in my side.

It's that word *willing*. That's the one I always get hung up on. I consider what I think I know about that word, the ways I use it. I picture a person with a strong will; I think of things I am willing or unwilling to do. A strong-willed child will not do what they do not want to do. And so I guess I always thought the leper was saying, "Lord, I know you can heal me, if you want to."

But it turns out I didn't know very much about that word *willing*. I thought it meant "want to." But it has a much deeper meaning, one that involves words like *purpose* and *intention*.[7]

So actually, the man was saying, "If it serves your greatest purpose, I know you can heal me. If you, in your wisdom and master intentions, see a purpose in healing me, please do it."

It wasn't about "want to." Jesus may very well want to give or heal or say yes, the same way—but to a far greater measure—that I will always want to give extravagantly to the people I love. I would love to say yes to my children every time they ask, but all those "yesses" would not produce people of character, diligence, perseverance, and patience. Parenting is one long marathon of acting toward and according to a greater purpose. On a much grander and more important scale, I can trust that God's no is according to his greater purpose, even if he's the one only who knows exactly how that no fits into his plan.

I cannot pretend to know or understand how or why some miracles happen and others do not. But I choose to believe with my entire being that God's eternal purpose is at the heart of all his decisions. While it makes little sense to me, perhaps it is true that there is sometimes greater eternal purpose in illness—and even in death—than there could be in a temporary healing. Sometimes I forget that this world is not all there is. And that's when I forget that there can be eternal purpose in the word *no*.

What could that purpose be? Maybe we do not get what we ask for because there is greater beauty in how we love each other when we don't get what we want. After all, anybody can be nice in a season of constant yes. Maybe Jesus wants to show his intimacy in the valley of what we do not have here, so when we meet him at last, finally face-to-face, we will know the one we've been talking to all these years.

I'll be honest: It feels like dangerous territory to even write these words. I feel like I am dancing on a thin tightrope stretched between two extremes: speaking for God or offering empty platitudes. Both ends of the spectrum, while filled with good intentions, can be terribly painful to the one listening.

Here's what I know: I trust who God is, even when I'm tired of waiting. I trust who he is, even when I have no idea what he is doing. When I ask for big things, I always believe he can, but I often wonder if he will. These two statements can live together in the same sentence. They can be sisters in the same house. One does not negate the other. I am allowed to do both.

Take heart, dear friend. Don't lose your courage. Don't give up. Don't stop asking for the desire of your heart. Come as close as the leper came. Ask with the humility he showed. And ask the Lord to open your eyes and your mind to the greater purposes in his answer.

Stay in it. Keep asking. There will come a day when all the waiting will make sense, even if it's not now, not in this lifetime, and not on this side of heaven. You and I will realize that these names and needs we kept presenting were never out of his sight or out of his hands. We will see what we couldn't see.

And at one of those dinner parties in heaven, I hope for a seat at the table reserved for the persistent widows.

. . .

Most things will be okay eventually, but not everything will be. Sometimes you'll put up a good fight and lose. Sometimes you'll hold on really hard and realize there is no choice but to let go. Acceptance is a small, quiet room.

CHERYL STRAYED, BRAVE ENOUGH

CHAPTER 15

Just You Wait

As You Go

In my final week of writing this book, I met with my friend Star to clear my mind a bit. Star has a red pixie haircut like Tinker Bell, and her freckles are sprinkled like paprika across her nose. Her name suits her: She straight up sparkles. I was bogged down in outlines and ideas and questions, and Star is a fellow writer who knows how to think things through. But our time together hardly cleared my mind.

As I told her what I was working on, she asked, "Do you know where you fit in this story? Do you know where you emerged on your side of the wait? Do you know what the wait was for?"

Leave it to a fellow writer to dig in and ask hard questions in the final stretch of the book you have to finish by Thursday.

I could feel anxiety rising from my toes, creeping up from under the table. *What are any of the answers?* It could be that I was mentally exhausted from the writing process, because there comes a point when you're pretty sure you can't get any more juice out of this orange. (The writer being the orange, just so we're clear.) But I honestly couldn't think of a single answer. And suddenly, I felt like a fraud. My mind was scrambling with self-doubt and insecurity. *Why am I writing a book about waiting when it appears that I don't know the first thing about it?*

I almost called my editor to say, "Forget it. I was wrong. Let's scrap this stupid idea. Let's write a cookbook."

Usually, when we can't find answers, we would rather not deal with the questions. That's how I felt when Star asked me these deep questions that made me question every page of the journey: *I do not know. Stop asking me hard things.*

But given a good night's sleep and a little space from the manuscript, I remembered. Oh, yes, that's the hard thing about waiting: There aren't answers. There isn't a map. Sometimes there's nothing you can do. And that's the scary and maddening thing about it: You don't know where you're headed or what this is for or about, or where and when it will end, or what it will even look like.

I completely love the GPS apps on my phone. My mind serves me in a lot of ways, but way-finding is not one of my strengths. Insert: All the driving apps. I'll admit, but I won't apologize: I'm spoiled by them. Do you remember the days, even if only in childhood, when the person in the passenger seat held the giant map with the route highlighted in yellow marker, and the only possible way to know "how much longer" was to guess at the distance between your fingertips? Detours and construction sure didn't show up on that map, so your trip could be suddenly delayed by hours, and there was almost nothing to be done about it. Those days are over; now we can know for reasonably certain that we will reach our destination in two hours and twenty-one minutes, and if there is an ever-so-slight change in that plan, the GPS will quickly inform us.

But making our way through this road trip of life seems to be more of the old-fashioned map variety. "Looks like I should go this way. Maybe that's the best plan, but I can't know for sure, and I can't tell where I would find any Starbucks on this route." Give me my trusty apps, complete with updates and icons and police alerts, thank you very much.

Waiting feels hard because we aren't in control. We are living in a time when something is wrong every single day. Hurricanes. Investigations. Allegations. Another mass shooting with another list of victims. Perhaps each year of being single on another birthday reminds us that we'd dreamed of being married by this age. Other years of wedding-anniversary dates remind us that we thought we would *still* be married at this age. There are diagnoses. Disappointments. Natural disasters. All reminders of how very little we can truly control. When we lose control, we get terrified quickly. And even if we can trust and believe that God is in control, we may not like how he is driving this bus we're all in together.

I cannot make you believe he is good. But I can only trust the sovereignty of God because I also trust the sweetness of Jesus. He is not a flippant God without care for his children. He can see things we cannot see; he has information we do not have. If he says no, then I can choose to trust that this answer serves for a greater plan—and maybe even my greater good—that I cannot see. When I cannot make sense of it, I can remind myself that I do not hold all the pieces of this puzzle. And I can recall that he has always been with me, closer than my own breath, even when he didn't give me what I wanted. Even, and perhaps especially, when he gave me exactly what I didn't want.

I deeply love this verse: "You did not forget to punish the guilty or listen to the cries of those in need" (Psalm 9:12, CEV). Those first four words have captured my heart. *You did not forget.*

In the midst of the waiting seasons, and even in the midst of the seasons after the wait, I need to rest in this deep truth: God did not forget. Those four words prompted me to list the things my God has not forgotten. I discovered this practice is good for the soul, whether the sun is shining or not.

- You did not forget about me.
- You did not forget about Tucker.
- You did not forget about Tyler.
- You did not forget about my aching heart.
- You did not forget that my children were fatherless.
- You did not forget how I love to love.

- You did not forget that I was single, or even more importantly, a single mom.
- You did not forget that Peter longed to be set free from gripping addiction.
- You did not forget that children everywhere are hungry.
- You did not forget about the senseless violence that is happening all around us.
- You did not forget that you are the Lord of lords, the Prince of Peace.
- You did not forget that we are waiting for you.
- You did not forget your promises.
- You did not forget the sparrows.
- You did not forget to remember.

Make your own list. Say what your heart needs to know God remembers. In your honesty, may you make way for truth and new perspective.

- He has not forgotten your sadness.
- He has not forgotten that you still want a baby in your arms.
- He has not forgotten your cry for healing.
- He has not forgotten that you need a job.
- He has not forgotten that you have bills to pay.
- He has not forgotten that you long for a companion.
- He has not forgotten what you have lost.
- He has not forgotten our nation.

- He has not forgotten you've been betrayed.
- He did not forget about you.

Even as you wait, he has not forgotten.

You do not wait alone, and you do not wait for nothing. He did not forget.

When my friend Sheri visited Kenya a couple of years ago, she learned that the Kenyans' concept of time is very different from ours. They are never in a hurry. It's almost as though they have learned to refuse to be rushed. They are fully in this moment, doing what is now. Kenyans have a saying in Swahili: *Haraka Haraka Haina Baraka.* It means, "Hurry by hurry, and the blessing is lost."

Lift your head, oh patient one. Look for the blessing in the now. The whole earth is full of God's glory, so keep your eyes wide open. Waiting is a time for watching. May the God Who Sees open your eyes to see glimpses of his work beneath the soil and behind the scenes.

The long days that feel empty and useless, the lists of questions without answers—they will become something. The jobs you must work before you get the one you're waiting for. The people you will date before you find the one you're waiting for. The pages in your journal that hold your many questions. The long walks of wondering and wandering.

These are making you. These are your becoming.

Just you wait.

. . .

Lord, today You know what I need to do.
But You can do more in my waiting than in my
doing I can do.
"TO THOSE WHO WAIT," BETHANY DILLON

For he will complete what he appoints for me,
and many such things are in his mind.
JOB 23:14, ESV

Reflections on Awakening

. . .

- Picture yourself in the throne room of God, the place where you can meet him in your imagination. Maybe it is a grand cathedral with stained-glass windows, paintings, and pews. Maybe it is a peaceful meadow beside a quiet stream. Maybe it's in a coffee shop, on a baseball field, or in a quiet corner of your bedroom. Let yourself imagine what it can look like, and let it be a place you can return to anytime you want to feel close to the one who knows you best.

- In your waiting, do you feel forgotten? Feelings are true but not always accurate; they are valid ways to describe your emotions, but they do not always represent accurate facts. Sometimes we must remind our feelings what we know to be true. Be intentional to speak truth to yourself, just as you would to someone you love.

- We sow seeds each time we are honest in our conversations with the Lord. Acknowledge the ways you feel forgotten. Make your list. Address each item you have written down. Give each one time and attention, as longing deserves to be named. Be honest with the Lord, and say what you really mean. He is patient with our honesty; that's where healing begins.

- Look again at each item on your list. Remind yourself what is true: He has not forgotten. Take your time with each memory and sit with the many pieces. Know this: In his remembering, he holds them all.

- *Haraka Haraka Haina Baraka.* "Hurry by hurry, and the blessing is lost." Take time to slow down today. Ask the Lord to help you become aware of the gifts he has given you, especially the ones you might have missed by hurrying through your day. What sights, smells, and sounds did you enjoy because you slowed down to hold the blessings?

- Look at the time line of your life. Choose three events, and record how God was present in the story, even if you can only see it now, in the fullness of the rearview mirror.

- Your story is unfolding in three layers:

  1. the story God is writing,
  2. your story without him, and
  3. the story you can write together.

  Ask God to help you weave these layers together so you can see your story, hear it, and tell it.
  The world needs to hear it.

Epilogue

For the past three years, I have attended an AA meeting on Peter's "birthday," the anniversary when he celebrates another year without a drink. I especially love to go to his morning meeting. Before the sun comes up, while the air is dark and cool, the parking lot fills with the cars of people on their way to work. They come inside to their room downstairs, to the sacred space where everyone is safe and welcome. They welcome one another with those faithful cups of coffee, and they start the day together.

They each begin with, "Hi, I'm _____, and I'm an alcoholic." They share their truth with one another, nuggets of honesty and wisdom that are carrying them through the next twenty-four hours. In keeping with the tradition of the anonymous program, I have asked permission to share the beauty of what I heard.

M. said, "Can I tell you what I'm enjoying about being sober? Just being kind to people. Kindness is a big deal, and I love it. I wake up in the morning, and I know that all I have to do is God's will for me . . . without drinking. So that's all I'm trying to do. I'm just trying to do God's will without a drink. And I'm pretty happy to be here today."

B. said, "When I stick with the program, people say things about me that I'm not used to. Last week, someone told me I'm calm, and I never knew that. The thing is, when you stick with the program, the good stuff kind of sneaks up on you. You don't realize you're changing and growing, but you are."

E. said, "I've discovered something really important: I can't trust my own brain. It tells me I need alcohol, but I don't. I can't trust it, and I don't have to listen to it. And that's revolutionary."

K. said, "You have to go out and share the hope with somebody. And the important thing is that the person who needs to hear it might not be somebody new to the program. We all need to hear it. We all need to be reminded."

D. said, "I'm thankful that the worst days don't last forever. And I've learned that the worst days are not the days for self-analysis. You don't have to figure out why you're struggling then, you just have to get through that day—without a drink. A few days later? That's when you can say, 'Man, why was I such a wreck on Thursday?' Then you can see clearly.

Don't try to figure out what's wrong while it's still dark. Wait for the fog to clear."

These people know truth. And they've fought for this wisdom.

Peter said, "Today is my birthday." And the room filled with applause.

"Seven years without a drink, you guys. Here I am, with my bride." Under the table, he put his hand on my knee. "And let me tell you, the greatest gift in my life is that this woman next to me will never have to see me drunk. So I'll keep coming back until they run out of chips or until I run out of breath."

L. said, "I remember when you first shared your story on your first birthday of sobriety. You had your story down, for sure. You sure were funny . . . but you sure weren't broken yet. Now you are funny, and you have the years to support your brokenness and your healing. Congratulations, Peter."

D. said, "Congratulations on your seven-year chip, Peter. I had one of those once."

Before Peter received his new bronze chip with a VII marked boldly on one side, they passed it around the room. Each person held it in their hands and closed their eyes. Each one blessed Peter's journey and every day of his seven years in whatever way made sense to them. They were celebrating his rebirth. The beginning of his new life, seven years ago. They are in this together, and a victory for one of them is a victory for all of them.

A. said, "Let me tell you how it feels to belong to this

group: It makes me feel safe. Coming here every day is the best thing about my morning. I don't have to believe in anything, I don't have to pay anything, and I don't even have to deserve to be here. I can just be here."

I cried as he said that: *I don't even have to deserve it.*

As a guest in this meeting, I listened, and I didn't say a word. But I cried quietly, so convicted by the fact that this is what the church should be. People who have come together to talk about what is hard, what is real, and what is true, and then to encourage each other to go out and let others know about the hope they have found.

Imagine what it could be like if we started all our conversations with words like "I'm Tricia and I'm a sinner." And then, what if the whole room responded with "Hi, Tricia." Because it's okay, and me too, and you're welcome here, sinner.

As they finished their meeting, I felt like I had been to church. The people in that basement, huddled together with their Styrofoam cups and their open books, they are the warriors. They are the heroes on the front lines. And their time together is the truest church I've been to.

· · ·

Peter unpacked his whole story for me on the back porch of the mountain house, in the old, wooden family rocking chairs overlooking the river. I rested my head back and rocked my chair in time with his. "So, what do you believe was the purpose of your wait?"

He paused, deep in thought.

"Well, the wait needed to happen in order to curb my selfishness. I think back on those days of strolling through the field with the six-pack of beer, aware that maybe I should cut back. I asked God to set me free, but *my God knows me.* I was never going to just put it down and walk away. If he let me off the hook again, I'd find another rule to break. I'm a stubborn guy, babe. I needed harsher circumstances and strict punishment. *My God knows me.*"

Peter grew silent as he gathered his thoughts, then continued. "It wasn't just about the threat of federal prison, though I thought it was. He knew what it would take for me to truly understand, accept, and come to terms with the prisons I had created for myself. Sure enough, it was an abrupt, hard stop. God had to wrestle my stubborn will away from me. I was a very selfish person. All of us are selfish, but addicts are more selfish than most, and selfishness is a prison of its own. That wait needed to happen to curb my selfishness."

"What do you think you learned?" I asked, pressing the boundaries of this sacred space in his heart.

Another long pause.

"I had to learn that this life wasn't all about me. I had to learn how to surrender. I mean, at times I'm still as selfish and whiny as a six-year-old. 'What about me, God? Sure, you saved me from driving drunk a thousand times, and you got me out of jail, and you stopped me from drinking—oh, and you gave your Son to save my soul. But other than that stuff, how about this other thing that I want?' Every single day, I'm still facing new reminders of my old self, that this life isn't about me and what I want. I like to think I'm waiting on God, but the reality is, often he's waiting for me."

This man. His heart.

It all blows me away.

We sit in silence as we fathom how different our lives are because God chose to write the story for us and with us. I thought of what we call the Polaroid Game: If someone came and snapped a Polaroid of this scene, and then if they somehow traveled back in time to show it to us—five, six, or seven years ago—how would we possibly connect the dots between what we knew then and what was waiting for each of us? The path was long and winding, dark and lonely. But it led us here. There had been gifts in the waiting all along.

Finally, I asked him, "What would you say to the person who doesn't understand why God won't set him or her free from addiction?"

"Somewhere," he said, "deep in their soul, in a place even deeper than they may be aware, they believe they need this addiction. They are convinced that their need is worse than anyone who has ever found sobriety.

"If you're ready to quit, you can quit," he added, his voice quiet and somber with remembering. "I had to wait because I still wasn't ready. I wasn't ready for freedom, healing, and surrender. I would say they're not free because they haven't surrendered.

"Anyone can say they want to cut back, or they want to stop altogether, but recovering from an addiction requires a shift from your head to your heart. The change is deep, and it is not easy. If you will do the work, you can make the heart change. God will do as much work as you will. He won't make you stop, but he will guide you. And he won't leave you.

"All he did was answer my prayer. I asked him to deliver me, but he knew I needed something a lot stronger than just a simple yes and a ride home. I wouldn't have learned with white-glove treatment. I needed a little surgery on my ego. Okay, major surgery. I thought he wasn't listening because he didn't do it the way I wanted, but not until the chaos settled could I see: He had been listening all along. He did *exactly* what I asked him to do."

"So, when we talked in the car," I said, "about the three stages of waiting—the Longing, the Becoming, and the Awakening—you said you didn't buy it. You said transformation doesn't just happen, and a person doesn't necessarily become anything different through the journey of waiting. Do you still think that? Because that story you just told me, that's pretty transformational."

"Transformation needs a catalyst: an action needs to start the reaction. So yes, longing will do that. I was separated from my family, from my bed, from my license to drive, from my freedom to make my own decisions. Trish, the fact that somebody who liked to party all the time would just . . . stop? And now to realize that I can have just as much fun as before—and I can remember it—and have a real life too. That's freedom. That's what that is. It's not just a transformation. It's *radical* transformation."

I read somewhere that humility is being transparent about the qualities you're still working on. And with Peter's story in my hands, I'd venture to say that humility is the most attractive quality there ever could be.

"Tell me," I said, reaching for his hand, "what is your life like now?"

Okay, yes, I was unabashedly fishing for compliments, but I truly wanted to hear this man I loved contrast his life now, our love, our family—with his life then.

He took my hand, rubbing his thumb across my knuckles, turning my wedding ring between his fingers. "Well, now I have you. For the first time in my life, I have someone who needs me. I have a wife. She listens to me. She loves me. And we never stop talking."

It's true. We don't.

. . .

For he wounds, but he also binds up;
he injures, but his hands also heal.
JOB 5:18, NIV

Acknowledgments

Writing is an act of solitude that stretches across hours of time alone with my coffee cup and earbuds. But a book is never written by just one person. I am unspeakably thankful for the people who surround me, strengthen me, and keep me in the game.

I thank my agent, Greg Johnson, a gentle shepherd and a fearless champion of my gifts. Greg is the keeper of my ideas and the messenger of good news. He clears the path, leads the way, and keeps me on track.

I thank the outstanding team at NavPress, most especially Don Pape, publisher extraordinaire; Jen Phelps, designer of a creative cover that perfectly captured the message of waiting with anticipation; and Elizabeth Schroll, meticulous copy editor who combs my writing with matchless precision.

I thank Caitlyn Carlson, my editor, who understands me implicitly. Some authors send their editor a curated manuscript that's perfect, polished, and complete. I faithfully send Caitlyn a hot mess and a thank-you note. She sculpts my piles of sand into castles, and her friendship is a gift to me.

I thank the community of Alcoholics Anonymous, the tribe of warriors who are saving each other every single day. You are the church.

I thank the pastors and teachers who have taught me the fruits of patience, the gifts in the stillness, and that waiting is a big deal to God. Phil Vaughan, Donna Vaughan, Krissy Hanna, Geoff Surratt, Ben Patterson, Craig Smith, and Steve Garcia are among the best communicators I know. Their teachings are sprinkled in these pages, and they have seasoned my life.

I thank my mom, my first reader who forever strengthens my sentences with questions, conversations, and wisdom. She makes everything better.

I thank my dad, who doesn't love to read, but who doesn't skip over a single word I write. Every girl deserves a dad like this one.

I thank my sons, Tucker and Tyler, my athlete and my artist. You are young men now, and you hold pieces of my heart that nobody else can ever claim. You make me think, you make me laugh, and you are my sunshine when clouds are gray. I will never get over the gifts of you. I'm crazy about you knuckleheads.

I thank Jack and Natalie, who let me love their dad. Jack is a man of wisdom and courage, a listener who can do hard things. Natalie is a warrior and a finisher, a woman of strength and fortitude and smarts. You are the bonuses I didn't know I needed.

I thank Peter, who holds my heart and all my pieces. He carries my books and burdens, he makes a perfect cup of morning coffee, and he will forever be my favorite miracle. I love you completely, Peter Heyer. (Can you believe we're *married*?)

And I thank readers of my books and my blog, the very many who said, "You're writing a book on waiting? Can you hurry up and finish?" I am thankful for the invisible sea of you who let my story and my life spill into yours. You keep me writing.

Notes

INTRODUCTION: HURRY UP AND WAIT
1. Genesis 1:1.
2. Luke 2:6.
3. Original idea found in *When the Heart Waits: Spiritual Direction for Life's Sacred Questions* by Sue Monk Kidd. She calls this the threefold cycle of waiting: separation, transformation, and emergence.
4. Jonah 1–2.
5. Exodus 38:26 says the Israelites had more than 600,000 mature males, and it doesn't record the number of women and children. Tradition estimates at least two million Israelites migrated from Egypt to Canaan.
6. Wayne Blank, "Taking the Long Way Home," Daily Bible Study, accessed December 20, 2018, http://www.keyway.ca/htm2002/20020720.htm.

CHAPTER 1: THE WAIT YOU'RE IN
1. 2 Corinthians 1:8-9.

CHAPTER 2: THE GREAT WAITERS
1. Genesis 2:19-20.
2. Genesis 6–8.
3. Genesis 16:1-6.
4. Luke 15:20.

5. See Daniel 6:16-23 (*Daniel*); 1 Samuel 22:1-5; Psalm 57; Psalm 142 (*David*); Exodus 2:11-25, AMP (*Moses*); Genesis 12:1-4; 17:15-17; 21:1-3 (*Abraham and Sarah*); Genesis 37:2; 39:1-23; 41:46 (*Joseph*); and Acts 23:23–25:11; 28:1-31 (*Paul*).
6. Job 19:23-27.
7. Psalm 57 and Psalm 142 were written while David was in the cave.

CHAPTER 4: LONGING TO BEGIN
1. "How Many Animals Were on Noah's Ark?" Ark Encounter, accessed January 16, 2019, https://arkencounter.com/animals/how-many/.
2. See 1 Corinthians 11:1.

CHAPTER 5: WHERE IS THE SUNSHINE?
1. John 14:3, NIV.

CHAPTER 6: WALKIE-TALKIE THEOLOGY
1. Matthew 4:1-11.
2. Luke 3:22.
3. Isaiah 41:10, ESV.
4. Isaiah 43:1.
5. Romans 12:2.

PART TWO: BECOMING
1. Marney Makridakis, "Kronos & Kairos: Linear and Numinous Time Concepts," Creativity Portal, accessed January 16, 2019, http://www.creativity-portal.com/articles/marney-makridakis/kronos-kairos-time.html#.XCaJoFxKjIU.

CHAPTER 7: HONESTY IN THE WAITING
1. Psalm 13:1, NIV.
2. Psalm 35:17, NKJV.
3. Psalm 94:3, CSB.
4. Jason Hague, *Aching Joy* (Colorado Springs: NavPress, 2018), 41.
5. Lysa TerKeurst, Twitter, February 24, 2018, https://twitter.com/LysaTerKeurst/status/967580671383359488.

CHAPTER 8: THE FRAT HOUSE, MEDITATION, AND TESTICLES
1. *Double-edged sword*: Hebrews 4:12; *pure and perfect*: Psalm 18:30; *light your path*: Psalm 119:105; *set you free*: John 8:32.
2. 1 John 4:4.

3. Psalm 48:9.
4. Psalm 145:5.
5. Psalm 119:27.
6. Joshua 1:8.
7. Joshua 1:9.
8. Psalm 121:1-2, NIV.

CHAPTER 9: PASSING TIME WITH A PEN
1. Mark Batterson, *The Circle Maker: Praying Circles around Your Biggest Dreams and Greatest Fears* (Grand Rapids: Zondervan, 2011, 2016).
2. Batterson, *Circle Maker*, 12.

CHAPTER 10: STOP LOOKING AT THE CLOCK
1. Ann Voskamp, Facebook, October 12, 2018, https://m.facebook.com/AnnVoskamp/posts/2220907357921426.

CHAPTER 11: SPARROWS AND A TATTOO
1. Psalm 84:3.
2. Matthew 10:29.
3. Luke 12:6.
4. Matthew 10:31.
5. Hosea 2:19-20, NIV.
6. Isaiah 41:13, GNT.
7. Exodus 29:42; 25:22.
8. Jack Hayford, "A Time of Altars," Jack Hayford Ministries, accessed January 16, 2019, https://www.jackhayford.org/teaching/articles/a-time-of-altars/.
9. *Ya'ad*. See https://www.bibletools.org/index.cfm/fuseaction/Lexicon.show/ID/H3259/ya\ad.htm.
10. The Greek word for "betrothed" used in Exodus 29:42 is *mnésteuó* (Bible Hub, s.v. "3423. mnésteuó," accessed January 2, 2019, https://biblehub.com/greek/3423.htm), which shares the root *mnaomai* with *mimnéskó*, "to remember" (Bible Hub, s.v. "3403. mimnéskó," accessed January 2, 2019, https://biblehub.com/greek/3403.htm).

PART THREE: AWAKENING
1. Mark 11:23-24, author's paraphrase.

CHAPTER 13: SEEDS IN THE GROUND, BUTTERFLY IN THE COCOON
1. Trina Paulus, *Hope for the Flowers* (Mahwah, NJ: Paulist Press, 1972), 76.

2. Luke 6:21.
3. Psalm 126:3, 5.
4. Psalm 126:6, NIV.
5. Psalm 56:9.
6. Psalm 57:7.
7. Lamentations 3:57, NIV.
8. Psalm 116:7.
9. 2 Timothy 1:12.

CHAPTER 14: THE ANSWER WE DON'T WANT
1. Luke 18:1-8.
2. *Merriam Webster's Thesaurus*, s.v. "persistent," accessed January 4, 2019, https://www.merriam-webster.com/thesaurus/persistent.
3. Luke 18:4-5, NIV.
4. 1 Thessalonians 5:17, ESV.
5. Mark 5:34, NIV.
6. Luke 5:12-13.
7. *Baker's Evangelical Dictionary of Biblical Theology*, s.v. "will (n.)," Bible Study Tools, accessed January 16, 2019, https://www.biblestudytools.com/dictionary/will/.

THE NAVIGATORS® STORY

THANK YOU for picking up this NavPress book! I hope it has been a blessing to you.

NavPress is a ministry of The Navigators. The Navigators began in the 1930s, when a young California lumberyard worker named Dawson Trotman was impacted by basic discipleship principles and felt called to teach those principles to others. He saw this mission as an echo of 2 Timothy 2:2: "And the things you have heard me say in the presence of many witnesses entrust to reliable people who will also be qualified to teach others" (NIV).

In 1933, Trotman and his friends began discipling members of the US Navy. By the end of World War II, thousands of men on ships and bases around the world were learning the principles of spiritual multiplication by the intentional, person-to-person teaching of God's Word.

After World War II, The Navigators expanded its relational ministry to include college campuses; local churches; the Glen Eyrie Conference Center and Eagle Lake Camps in Colorado Springs, Colorado; and neighborhood and citywide initiatives across the country and around the world.

Today, with more than 2,600 US staff members—and local ministries in more than 100 countries—The Navigators continues the transformational process of making disciples who make more disciples, advancing the Kingdom of God in a world that desperately needs the hope and salvation of Jesus Christ and the encouragement to grow deeper in relationship with Him.

NAVPRESS was created in 1975 to advance the calling of The Navigators by bringing biblically rooted and culturally relevant products to people who want to know and love Christ more deeply. In January 2014, NavPress entered an alliance with Tyndale House Publishers to strengthen and better position our rich content for the future. Through *THE MESSAGE* Bible and other resources, NavPress seeks to bring positive spiritual movement to people's lives.

If you're interested in learning more or becoming involved with The Navigators, go to www.navigators.org. For more discipleship content from The Navigators and NavPress authors, visit www.thedisciplemaker.org. May God bless you in your walk with Him!

Sincerely,

DON PAPE
VP/PUBLISHER, NAVPRESS